A Cheesecake Christmas

Deb Goodman

Contents

Join Deb's newsletter to get the book, *Love in Reality*, totally free!

https://bit.ly/3DtjnSU

https://debgoodmanwrites.com

To my mom.

I love and appreciate you.

Chapter 1

Aria

May

Camilla's Wedding

The reverend marrying my best friend and her sweetheart has black sideburns and a jawline that remind me of Elvis, and I can't stop staring.

No, she didn't choose an actual Elvis impersonator to marry them. That's not quite the vibe she was going for.

But true to Camilla's personality, the wedding does have a few quirky surprises, like her flowerless bouquet, which is a mix of natural, dark green leaves so enchanting that, after seeing it, I wonder why anyone would ever choose a bouquet *with* flowers. It's a masterpiece of greenery, with some leaves even dipped in gold.

It's not a flowerless wedding, though, and the mix of pink and purple hyacinths and tulips throughout the chapel and in my bouquet provide a sweet, earthy scent.

"You are now man and wife," the reverend announces in a raspy, very un-Elvis-like voice. "You may kiss the bride."

Camilla's catcall punctuates the air in the white stone chapel in New Hedge, Colorado. There's a smattering of laughter amongst the attendees as Jesse dips her low, kissing her soundly.

Like, really soundly. And when he tries to ease up, Camilla grabs the lapel of his three-piece blue and black tweed suit and smashes his lips against hers again, eliciting another round of laughter.

As maid of honor, I have the perfect view of the action, as well as of Jesse's younger brother Theo, the best man, who keeps catching my gaze from the other side of the aisle. Maybe it's the sentimentality in the air, or his earnest and uncharacteristically shy smile, but I can't help but glance back.

I normally have little to do with Theo, ever since he came on too strong when we first met at Camilla's bakeshop, Shorty's, a year and a half ago. The man is an unapologetic flirt, and when he asked me what was good on the Shorty's menu with a cringy "Besides you. I bet you're good," I saw red. I've been trying to avoid him ever since.

But today? He's been a conscientious best man, taking care of such things as running home to get Jesse's forgotten tie and cheerfully helping the guests get settled in the pews.

And we seem to both be dateless to this wedding, which somehow helps. My long-distance boyfriend, Rob, had to cancel his airline ticket from Arkansas last minute, which leaves me vulnerable. Alone.

And nervous, because he said he'd hoped we could have a conversation when he was here. Which sounded serious. Rob and I don't usually do serious.

I figured this would all come to the surface at Camilla's wedding. All day, my emotions have me feeling like I'm perched on one of those wobble balance boards. It's thrilling, but I'm clenching every muscle in my body, willing myself not to fall on my behind. Camilla's been my best friend since we were kids. The smallest thought or whiff of a memory has me pitching to one side, my arms flailing in wild circles, my mouth cursing at myself to *Get a grip*!

I'm happy she found Jesse. They're perfect for each other. He's the sensible peas to her loud, paprika-spiced carrots. But Camilla and I have been best friends for so long that it's strange to have things shift so drastically.

To the strains of Frank Sinatra's "Come Fly with Me," Camilla holds hands with Jesse, skipping up the aisle in her soft white, A-line dress with a square neckline and sheer bishop's sleeves. With every hop, her lavender Vans sneakers are visible, making me smile.

When they near the tall, dark brown double doors, Theo offers me his arm, his grin cocked to one side, his brows raised in a question. I weave my arm through his, the mint and wintry evergreen scent of his cologne hitting me.

He's a tall, handsome, blue-eyed man. Why shouldn't I enjoy his company today?

We walk, no skipping for us, and it's fine. Maybe even nice.

He leans in close to my ear. "I thought bridesmaids dresses were often second rate, but this?" His gaze takes in my blush-colored A-line scoop chiffon dress. "You look unreal."

It's Theo. He flirts with everyone, including Camilla's Grammy. But right now, I breathe it in, roll around in it like a cat in catnip, and find myself pressing the length of my upper arm against his. It's a nice upper arm. With the attendees all standing and getting ready to head outside, no one's paying any attention to us anyway.

Except for the blonde, leggy model who joins us as we exit the church.

"Good job up there, Theodore," she says in a European accent I can't place, before planting a wet, loud kiss on his cheek. I extricate myself from his arm, and his gaze goes back and forth between us like he's torn between obligation—me—and her—the uncommonly gorgeous woman who's wearing a short, poufy babydoll dress that's so light pink, it could easily be mistaken for white.

White. At a wedding. My best friend's wedding.

To be fair, it isn't white. But it *seems* white, and that's not okay.

The swoony air between them isn't okay, either. I feel like I've intruded into their own personal romance novel.

"I'm Gelsey," she says to me. She leans her arm on Theo's shoulder and extends the other one for me to shake.

"This is Aria, the maid of honor. And Aria, this is my friend, Gelsey." Theo's cheeks hold the slightest flush, which could be considered cute, attractive even, in another time and place.

"Nice to meet you." I leave out the blistering repeat of the word "friend" that's lodged in my brain. I shake her hand, and it's as soft and smooth as a rose petal.

Of course.

I offer them both a brief smile and turn away, trying and failing to move along. We step outside, but there's some bottlenecking going on in the line of guests who've exited the church. And everyone's supposed to start milling over to the reception on the lawn around the back, but they're all talking and laughing amongst themselves.

Isn't it Theo's unofficial job to direct them? To get them moving?

I squint in the bright, late afternoon, spring sun and bring my hand up to shade my eyes, looking for an exit strategy. It's not like I want to ask Theo to say something to them. I can do it myself.

Just as I find a hole in the crowd that I can snake through, I overhear Gelsey behind me. "What do you think of my dress?" she asks Theo.

"It's so good," he responds playfully, and instantly, I'm back at the bakeshop when he said something similar to me, the same velvety layers in his voice.

Alrighty then.

Theo is actually the same as always. A womanizer to the core.

And I guarantee he'll never change.

The next day, I restock the glass display case at Shorty's Bakeshop, where I've worked ever since Camilla took ownership three years ago. I'm still tired from the wedding, but it's nothing I can't handle.

Besides, the memories of Camilla on her big day have me grinning. Every part of the wedding screamed Camilla: happy and unexpected, like the finely detailed fondant groom's cake that she made to look like Jesse's dog, Moose. And her dress was perfect for her, flowy enough to accommodate her animated movements.

It was Theo and his date who had me digging fingernail-shaped divots in my palms and in the stem of my bouquet ever since she appeared at Theo's side.

It wasn't so much her—Gelsey. I'm sure she's a lovely person. It was the way Theo interacted with her.

The focus is supposed to be on the bride and groom, Theo, not you and your woman of the month.

The whole thing had me scratching my head, especially because he came into the bakeshop not two weeks ago with a *different* woman.

Camilla's on her honeymoon in Bermuda, so I can't exactly talk to her about this stuff. Besides, Theo's officially her brother-in-law now. Is there some sort of rule for this kind of thing? Some etiquette around not bringing up your best friend's new in-laws in a less-than-flattering light?

I text my grandpa about the wedding. It's fun to explain the day like a story because I know he'll enjoy it. Besides, he's a great sounding board: non-judgmental, non-prescriptive, and he always makes me laugh.

Grandpa Beckwith texts back: *Sounds like this Theo is a menace. Want me to set him straight?*

I smile. I can always count on him to have my back, and to pick up on the parts that are a little sticky for me.

Me: *Nah. But thanks. I just needed to vent to someone about it.*

Grandpa Beckwith: *I guess we can only hope he gets coal in his stocking this year, huh?*

Me: *I'll cross my fingers. You're still planning on coming for Christmas, right?*

He's spent every other Christmas, on the even years when he's not with my mom's siblings, in New Hedge for as long as I can remember. The tradition involves him taking us to the Charles Dickens Christmas Festival at least a couple of times. When I was little, he'd always buy me something, like some handmade doll clothes or a jewelry box. Since I've become an adult, we split some candied almonds and spend an inordinate amount of time at the huge model trainset and village on display. He still makes up goofy stories about the tiny plastic people that litter the village, creating generational lines connecting them.

Grandpa Beckwith: *Of course. You think I want to be stuck in Boca Raton?*

Grandpa is my person—a breath of fresh air in my not-so-functional family. He says it like it is. He makes me laugh like no one else—and he adores me, but not in a fussy way.

Me: *Can't wait for you to get here!*

Grandpa Beckwith: *Let's see how many trips to the festival we can squeeze in.*

I hear the kitchen door behind me swing open and Danene's footsteps on the tile floor. "I'm finished up with the bread. You sure you don't need me to stay?" she asks.

With Camilla away on her honeymoon, it's fallen to Danene, Camilla's grandmother, and me to take turns holding down the fort.

"I'll be fine!" I'm looking forward to the peace and quiet of the early afternoon here. It will give me a chance to work on some of my design projects for my portfolio. I recently graduated with my second bachelor's—this one was an online marketing program. Someday, when I get the courage to branch out, I want to work for a brand management company.

Danene leaves and my head is down, which is probably why I don't notice I have customers until they're at the counter. They must have snuck in right as Danene left, which would explain why I didn't hear the bell above the door a second time.

"Aria?" Theo seems as surprised to see me as I am to see him. His blue eyes skate over me as he rapidly chews his gum.

I attempt to rearrange my features into a cool indifference, but my insides are rioting. Not only is Theo smug, but the arm of yet *another* woman is hooked around his.

This one's short and curvy, and her red hair hangs in a thick, straight sheet down to her waist.

My gaze goes from her to Theo. "Hey Theo, what's up?"

He's only scowling in confusion, so I turn to the woman. "Hello," I say to her. "What can I get for you?"

Beside her, Theo coughs and clears his throat, like he's choking on something. I try to ignore it, but he keeps coughing and choking.

"Oh my gosh. Do you have some water?" she asks me. She lets go of his arm and pounds on his back. It sounds like something went down the wrong tube.

I point to our small drink refrigerator in the corner by the counter. Theo's glance at me is wide-eyed with a sliver of apology.

While the woman turns to get him a water bottle, Theo's cough subsides enough for him to speak. He points to his throat. "I accidentally swallowed my gum." *Cough, cough.* "I didn't think you'd be in today." *Cough, cough.* "I thought it was Camilla's Grammy's turn."

I smooth my tangerine apron down with my palms, noticing how good this shade looks with my coloring. If the man has to see me in an apron, at least it's my best one.

My throat grows dry as my train of thought catches up to me. I do not care what Theo thinks of me, so I should wear all my rattiest aprons from now on, just to prove my point.

He starts to cough again. By now, the redhead is back, twisting off the lid and handing him the bottle of water. "You okay?" she asks, her brow furrowed. She reaches up and moves a lock of hair out of his eyes. The movement is intimate, as was the connection he had with the other woman only yesterday.

My palms grow slick, and my lungs are clogged with glue. Where does he get off, thinking he can lead these women on?

"I'm curious about your future plans," I say to him, my smile sardonic.

"Huh?" he asks between sips of water.

My upper lip curls, and I laugh. I've got him in my sights like an owl to a teeny, tiny, unsuspecting mouse.

"I'm just wondering if you're planning on bringing *all* your dates to the bakeshop?" I ask in a teasing voice.

His confused expression only deepens. I address the redhead. "His date at his brother's wedding yesterday? Gelsey, I think her name was? She's never come in here with him."

I offer a sympathetic smile. I don't want to make this woman feel bad. But she deserves to know, doesn't she?

"He brought someone else here a couple of weeks ago." I turn back to Theo. "She asked if I would scrape the chocolate icing off her eclairs before I wrapped them up. Remember?"

I'm still smiling, but the redhead lets out a sharp growl. She snatches the bottle away from him and sets it down roughly on the counter, sloshing water on the butcher block surface.

Her cheeks are fire engine red. "Theo?" she says to him, her voice spearing him with disdain.

He only works his jaw before letting out a pent-up breath and scrubbing the back of his neck.

She grabs the water bottle again and squeezes it with a pop, the contents of it shooting him in the face. He sucks in a soft gasp, and she whirls around and leaves the shop.

I'm rooted to the tile I'm standing on.

Because Theo's across from me, water dripping from his dark hair. The entire upper half of his lemon-yellow T-shirt is drenched.

But his expression has my cheeks burning as hotly as the redhead's.

His gaze is fixed upon me, his dark eyes wide. He's regarding me as if I'm a mermaid riding a dolphin bareback in an emerald sea—he's positively starstruck.

I open my mouth, but not a single word forms.

These last five minutes have not gone how I'd imagined.

And Theo is positively delighted.

Chapter 2

Theo

November

I might have overpromised and underdelivered. A little. Not something I wanted to do. But in an effort to talk my boss, Allen Weatherby, into buying this building for the law firm, I might have been looking at it through rose-colored glasses, my excitement affecting my good judgment.

Amidst the chatter of workmen and hammers in the next room, I scuff my foot across the floorboards. Is this cloud of dust new from the remodel, or old dust from the years it sat vacant until Weatherby bought it this past summer?

From the smell of it, it's old dust, but our replacement location has to be ready in a week. That's when the new owners take over our old place.

The carpets still haven't been installed. Which means the furniture isn't in. Which means Weatherby isn't happy.

Jay Knowles, his son-in-law and partner, is on a Caribbean cruise right now. Which also may have something to do with Weatherby's passive-aggressiveness lately—he's been filling in for Jay and is, therefore, busier than normal.

I sidestep around a bunch of paint rollers that were left here and make a mental note to ask the painters to pick them up. We've got to clear the floors for the carpet guys to come in and do their magic.

Why I'm Weatherby and Knowles' makeshift construction manager is something I can only hazard a guess at. But when you work for a law firm in New Hedge, Colorado, population 9,000, you have to work where you're needed. Especially when you're the new guy. Even though it's been three years, it feels like a title I'm never going to shake.

What? Someone needs to oversee the remodel of our new office?

Theo will do it.

There's a case with the district prosecutor defending a guy who's one hundred percent guilty and a scumbag?

Give it to Theo.

There's only space for two offices on the main floor, so someone needs to take the cramped one upstairs?

Theo's young and sprightly. He won't mind sprinting up and down the narrow, creaky staircase multiple times a day.

Not that it's terrible. The construction company has done a good job with the remodeling, and it's going to be a whole lot better than our current location, which we recently discovered has a mold problem. It looks fantastic, and my new office even has a little balcony. You can't beat the view of the New Hedge sunsets.

It's odd being responsible for this remodel. It was my idea in the first place, but I have zero say in the details.

A strange juxtaposition.

I text Weatherby some updates on the progress and put in a couple of phone calls to schedule the movers over the weekend. I'm a positive guy, so in my texts to Weatherby, I mostly focus on how nice the reception desk looks, *"like a hickory walnut utopia,"* I tell him.

Just as long as it isn't snowing the day we move in, we should be golden.

I take the stairs behind the reception desk two at a time to check out how things are looking up there. We've designated the upstairs as storage, my office, future offices, and a future rec room with a pool table and popcorn maker overlooking New Hedge.

That last bit was my idea since we all need to take some downtime once in a while. Weatherby and Jay plan to eventually bring on new attorneys, but the thought of the firm expanding has my head throbbing. I don't want any new people until I can be sure I'm on Weatherby's good side, solidifying myself as partner material.

But first, the grunt work. Which is why I'm here, enjoying the smell of fresh paint, which, fun fact, is a color called "Featherbed." Deference to the grunt work is also why I try to be the first person in the office every morning and the last one to leave.

I move to the future rec room at the front of the building and open the blinds. The brittle plastic snaps in two as I pull on the string.

I add "new blinds upstairs" to the list on my phone of things to do before the weekend, and then gaze out over the landscape below.

Except "landscape" is too fancy of a word. Storage units, as far as the eye can see, stretch on either side across the street, lines and lines of aluminum and concrete wasteland.

The downtown revitalization project should save our block of connected, rowhouse-style units from going the way of the masses. And I, for one, am excited about that. Something needed to stop the storage unit magnate from snatching up every little piece of the pie around here.

Out the window, I see a flash of movement.

It's Aria Robinson leaving out the front doors of the bakery, which is connected to our building.

It's not a surprise, since I know she works there as Camilla's graphic designer, social media manager, and marketer in one, but seeing her always jolts me, like that ice bucket challenge for ALS that made the rounds when I was a teen. Even though you're expecting the jolt, it still gets you every time.

She disappears, walking right next to the building, and then I hear a faint knock on the front door.

She's coming in here, and I need time to school my expression. I go down the stairs, much more slowly than I went up, taking my time and enjoying that with each step down, I can see more and more of the vision in front of me.

Her long, dark hair is pulled back in a colorful turban that acts as a hairnet when she's around the food in the bakeshop. She's in wide-legged, dark-washed jeans and a thin blue sweater, covered by a white apron. Her swan-like neck and her regal collarbones under smooth, tan skin come into view. I 've never thought of any woman's collarbones as being "regal," but that's the only way to describe Aria's.

Now I can see her eyes, right before I take the last step down. Large, luminous, velvety brown. Like Bambi, the baby deer. She even has the finest sprinkling of freckles across her cheeks, like spots on said baby deer. They are barely noticeable, but if you stand close to her, you can see them.

Not that I've gotten to stand close to her much. We're not exactly friends. I came on a bit too strong the day we met in the bakeshop two years ago. I'd been in my default mode, the I-can't-help-but-flirt-around-an-attractive-woman mode that I can't help getting in when I'm nervous. It was the completely wrong way to approach her, and I've been regretting it ever since.

"Theo." She says it like a confession—like she has no choice but to utter it.

"Hey, neighbor," I say as I reach her. I throw my arms wide. "What do you think of the new place, huh?"

Her gaze takes in the room. It's not done yet, but she should have seen it three months ago.

"I like it. The scent of new paint is top notch," she says.

"I know," I say. I scrunch up my face. "Is it wrong to love the smell of paint?"

She grunts a laugh. "If you're not actively seeking it out, it's probably fine." She nods as she steps forward to look around some more. "Camilla said you're moving in this weekend."

"We were. We are." I give a firm nod. "The carpet is going in tomorrow."

She shifts her weight to one side, and I know she's gearing up to say something I'm not going to like.

"Do you know who owns the Beemer that's illegally parked in the back?" Her nostrils flare.

I chuckle. I thought Camilla was the one who was dramatic. "It's not illegally parked, but—"

"It is. And our delivery guy can't get to where he needs to be."

"Well, I'll move it right away." I feel my phone vibrate and stretch out a finger to her before I answer it. I have to do a spin move to avoid two workers carrying the large beam that will become the fireplace mantel.

I answer the phone because it's Weatherby, but I don't miss Aria's huff and her arms crossing over her chest. If it had been anyone else calling, I would have silenced the call. But Aria does not understand the level of dedication Weatherby requires. He's not a bad guy or a bad boss, I just want to make his life easier in whatever way I can.

"Things are set up with the Fleming case," Weatherby tells me. "It's all yours. He's out on bail, so he can come to you."

"Great," I lie. It's not great. I don't want this case. Weatherby and Knowles is a full-service law firm. In a town this size, we have to be, and I love it. But there's a reason I don't practice in an inner city—I don't like criminal law.

Maybe I'm a bit too squeamish for that kind of thing. Give me adoptions, prenups, or wills . . . I don't like dealing with criminals. But Weatherby's a tennis pro on a world tour and I'm his ball boy, crouched, unseen in the corner by the net, poised to run across the court to retrieve anything and everything he needs.

Weatherby sighs through the phone. "Did you hear about the scandal with the Christmas festival? Something about the charity the co-hosts run being a scam?"

"No, I hadn't heard that."

"Well, my wife's in a tizzy. Says she feels betrayed by the co-hosts. She's worried people will boycott the festival."

"She volunteers, doesn't she?"

Weatherby growls. "Yes. She's always doing something or other to contribute. Anyway, we should keep our eye on this. They might need some legal help."

"Will do." I don't like drama. I'm a lover, not a fighter. But if the co-hosts of the festival have been scamming people, I have to do something to try to help.

"Oh, and can you send photos of this supposed utopia in reception?" Weatherby asks with a laugh. "Charlotte wants to see."

"Of course." I quickly send a few photos to both Weatherby and Charlotte, receptionist and legal secretary in one, and then end the call.

Only then do I turn back around to face Aria, whose gorgeous face has a frown.

"Your car? My guy is waiting."

Her guy? I know she means the teen I've seen hanging around the bakery the past couple of months, but it also reminds me that she actually does have a guy. A boyfriend. I think he lives in Arkansas. Why he's fool enough to live so far away from a woman like Aria beats me. If she were mine, I'd never do that.

She isn't mine. That doesn't mean there's zero percent chance that could ever change though, right?

I'm an optimist.

"Let me grab my keys." I spin around to our new reception desk, slide open the drawer and produce my keychain. Maybe if I keep talking to her, she won't leave yet. "Here, head out back with me and we'll see what's going on."

"You're going to need to talk to the city about getting your own parking spots back here. All these belong to Shorty's." She's in front of me as we walk past the stairs to the offices on either side of us. Thankfully, the freshly painted, glossy white trim and refurbished hardwood floors look great—nearly ready for Weatherby and Knowles to move in.

We step outside. "There's room over there for your parking," she says, her voice encouraging. "You'd need a striping company to come out."

"But you guys don't need—" I start to count. "Eight . . . nine parking spots."

"Yes, we do."

"I've never seen any other cars here besides yours and Camilla's. Okay, maybe Jesse's sometimes."

Jesse's my older brother. He married Camilla in the spring, and he's never been happier.

"Theo, our customers park back here all the time."

I give her a look. I know that's not exactly true. Most of the customers park out front near the street. I shrug. I can go easy on her this once. We'll leave the serious tones to Jesse. "I know I haven't been around much. But I will be very soon, and then I'll have a better idea of how parking shapes up around here."

"With your firm under construction, it's been extra crowded here. It's been a big problem." Aria steps in front of me to wave to the kid driving the delivery van. "Hang tight," she tells him. "Theo will be moving his Beemer soon."

There's an edginess between us. Thick unease is flinging off her like she's been dipped in oil.

I near my car and use the remote start, loving the purr of the engine. I tilt my head to the passenger's side as I open my door. "Want to get in for a bit?" Why do I torture myself like this? She doesn't want to get into my car for five seconds while I move it over a couple of spots.

"Maybe another time." She peers at her nails.

I move the car, and then she signals to the delivery kid to back into the spot I'd occupied before. I jump out, but before I can reach her side again, she's already unloading a cart from the back of the van.

"I thought you guys didn't do deliveries?" I ask, taking a hold of the opposite side of the rolling rack. I spin it around so I'm the one having to walk backwards. I notice the kid steering another one out. It's cold today, but he's only wearing a thin hoodie.

"We didn't used to. But with all our online orders, we needed someone to drive them over to the shipping company. Camilla figured if we were buying the van anyway, we could add a delivery service."

"That's great. Jesse said you're doing well these days."

Aria arches an eyebrow and raises her chin. "We are." Her gaze darts to the door that I know is looming behind me. I was staring at her so much I forgot to watch where I was going.

"I've got it from here," she says. "Thanks."

I open the door and hold it for her as she maneuvers past me. Her wrist, her skin so smooth and soft, brushes my own. An electric shock zips through me.

I know that my chemistry with Aria is off the charts. I've known it since I met her.

And like a glutton for punishment, I'm moving in next door to where she works. For what? To torture myself until she'll agree to go out with me?

Because that's all I need. She's gotten under my skin, and I don't like that I can't seem to crack the Aria code. I can't figure out what makes her tick. And yes, it bothers me that she doesn't like me.

Except, the weird thing is, somehow, Aria being mad at me is more pleasurable than any other woman being nice to me.

Chapter 3

Aria

I have to remove my apron and stand in front of the fan in the kitchen when I get back inside. Because Theo is like a little burr under the skin, and I'm overheating.

And continuing to think of him is a reflex that feels wrong.

Because, in theory, in some universe and in some way, I could like Theo.

In *theory*. But only because I'm now single.

Rob and I broke up several weeks ago.

Strangely, this hasn't been as difficult as I thought it would be. Rob gave me an ultimatum in the spring: move to Arkansas and get engaged, or we part ways.

I asked him for some time to think.

And I thought about it, all summer and into the fall, wondering if we kept things going a while longer if everything would become clear and a decision, one way or the other, would feel right. But when he brought it up again in September, I couldn't agree to it. We ended the conversation no longer together.

We'd been a couple for four years, so it wasn't a surprise that he asked me to make a decision. Rob's a good guy. Stable, safe, and loyal. But the thought of taking that next step filled me with such dread.

And that was the thing that made the decision for me: the dread.

"It's November." Camilla comes into the kitchen to help Elijah, our delivery guy, load up the carts with our shipments for the day. "No fans."

I shoot her a look. Yes, technically, she's my boss. But she's been my best friend for way longer. "Give me one minute. I've been dealing with Theo. Did you know he has a Beemer?"

"You didn't? He's had it for a while."

"I've never noticed, but it was blocking the van." I fan the bottom hem of my sweater in and out. "We've got to work out the parking with . . . what's the firm called again? Weatherby and—?"

"Knowles," Camilla supplies. "Weatherby and Knowles. A father-in-law, son-in-law type of deal. Well, father-in-law, son-in-law, and then Theo, the tagalong."

Something about Theo being a tagalong makes me laugh. It's a ridiculous notion because he has such a large presence. He could never be an afterthought. "And why are they moving in next door?" I shake my head. There aren't many lawyers in town, and I was surprised to hear that the firm Jesse's brother works for was one of the businesses taking part in the tax breaks and incentives that come with the downtown revitalization.

"Because they've had their old building since Weatherby's grandfather started the firm, apparently. It was small and in a bad location. They recently sold it."

"This location's not much better."

"Not yet anyway," Camilla chides. "But they're some of the brave souls who decided to take on this adventure to bring traffic over to this side of town. I, for one, am grateful to them. It can only help our business."

Yes. But at what cost?

I almost say that aloud, but then I think better of it. Camilla already knows that Theo and I are like oil and water. There's no sense mentioning it again.

Camilla rests her lower back against the counter. "Jesse suggested we expand our Christmas offerings. Our flagship shortbread is great, but he thinks adding something new for the holidays, something different from the shortbread, would bring in new customers."

"Huh. I like that idea. What did you have in mind?"

"Well, nothing. That's the problem. I can't think of anything special enough."

"Don't worry, Camilla. We'll come up with something good."

We finish helping Elijah load the carts, and Camilla gives him instructions. "Deliver the top two first. They're close to one another. And then go to the shipping company to send the rest off."

He's frowning, staring into the void, so Camilla repeats the instructions.

"Oh, and maybe you'd better start bringing your coat?" she says. "It's below freezing sometimes now."

He grimaces, but then covers it up with a nod and starts rolling the carts back to the van.

"Is he okay?"

She shrugs. "He's eighteen. That might be normal for an eighteen-year-old guy? I don't know."

"What did we ever do without him?" I ask Camilla.

"He's sweet," she agrees.

Running her grandfather's bakeshop has pushed her, but she's gotten into the swing of things. Along with our long-time bread maker, Danene, we have Elijah to do the deliveries, and Merre, a recent college grad who comes in to help fulfill orders and cashier.

That leaves Camilla and me more time to do what we do best. She bakes and does payroll. I manage the bills, marketing, and design.

It's the perfect system. But she knows I'd like to move on, at some point, to work in brand management—which would combine my graphic design major, my public relations minor, and my new bachelor's in marketing.

She fully supports me getting a corporate job. But it's hard for me to think of leaving what's comfortable.

Camilla sighs. "Elijah *is* the best. Always on time, reliable, polite. He's a good kid."

He's technically only six or so years younger, but that feels like a lot.

"I hope he has a coat," I say. "The look on his face when you mentioned it made me wonder."

"Me, too." She moves her thick blonde hair out of the way to rub her temple. "I could maybe offer him one of Jesse's old ones."

"It wouldn't hurt. Maybe hang it up in the back so he can grab it if he needs it. And he's been more withdrawn lately, don't you think?" I ask. She's still in newlywed-mode sometimes and might not have noticed.

She frowns. "Now that you mention it, yes. He does seem quieter. Like something's on his mind."

"Maybe he has girlfriend trouble. Would he ever open up to us?"

"The thought of him having a broken heart kills me," Camilla says, curling both fists to her throat.

"Let's keep a close eye on him. Maybe he'll talk about it eventually. Oh, and hey, I need to get off a little early tomorrow," I say.

"Sure," Camilla says. She and I have been partners in this business for long enough, it's not a problem for me to do what I need to do.

"The festival reached out to me, telling me they like my volunteer design work. They asked if I'd come to the committee meeting to-morrow night."

She tilts her head and hip to one side. "Seriously? That's a dream come true for you, right?"

"One of my earliest memories is those Christmas blazers." I can't help my smile. "And going to the festival when my grandpa would come to town for Christmas. He'd spoil my siblings and me rotten and buy us fun stuff, like those huge cinnamon rolls. I loved every second of it."

Camilla's brows go in the air. "Cinnamon rolls? What about offering cinnamon rolls during the Christmas season? Oh, or maybe dipped chocolates?"

"Either of those could work," I agree.

But my mind is still on the festival and the committee who runs it. Over their normal clothes, the committee members wear Christmas-printed suit coats showcasing an off-white background with ivy leaves, Christmas trees, snowflakes in shimmery blue, and red and white striped candy canes. In my childhood mind, they were the most mesmerizing jackets. Businessy, yet whimsical. Magical. A symbol of power and Christmas cheer.

And it wasn't just when I was a kid. I can own the fact that I still want one.

Normalize wanting to wear the tacky Christmas blazers!

"While you're there, you might as well tell them I've paid the entrance fee already," Camilla says, biting her bottom lip. "The finance person reached out, but I paid it a week ago."

"I know." I was the one who made the payment, technically. I remember how dicey it was at times two years ago. Because of a lack of finances and a fire in Camilla's garage, we weren't at all sure that Shorty's would be able to have a booth at the festival.

But they managed to find a booth that fit the bill. The festival, being all about Charles Dickens, requires the booths to look like they're buildings on an old London street. Many of the booths are set up in the renovated Barrie Mansion, now an events center, where walls were removed to expand the central grand ballroom. The rest of the booths are housed in a large event tent in the acre-sized backyard.

Being in the festival turned out to be a wise decision for Shorty's, bringing in more loyal followers of Camilla's seasonal shortbread and kicking off the new website with a bang. The business is getting there, thanks to Camilla's vision and hard work, as well as her husband Jesse's entrepreneurial expertise.

Merre enters the kitchen, tying up her golden-brown locks in one of those wide headbands. "Did you say something about the Christmas festival? That Charles Dickens one?"

Both Camilla and I nod and giggle. There isn't another festival worth mentioning, at least not to anyone in this community. We'll cut her some slack, though. She isn't a lifelong New Hedger like we are. She moved here after she graduated from college not long ago.

"Did you hear about the problem with the charity they've been donating to?" Merre asks. "Something about most of the money not even going to buying shoes for kids like they claimed?"

"No, I hadn't heard. That's too bad," Camilla says.

"Wait. Shoes and Dues doesn't actually donate much to the kids?" I don't want to believe that anything that has to do with the festival is untrustworthy.

Merre shrugs. "I heard that over ninety percent of the funds goes right back to the people who run the charity. The kids don't even get ten percent of it. And so some people are calling for a boycott of the whole festival."

At my dropped jaw, Merre takes a step back. "But who knows if it's true or not?"

It better not be. Nobody messes with the festival.

"Let us know if you hear anything else," Camilla says. "You'd think they'd address the issue with all those who'll have a booth. Aria, is this your grandpa's year to come to New Hedge?"

"Yes. I'm dying to see him."

"He's coming to the festival, right?"

"Always." If I can hang on until grandpa gets here, things might be okay. Having him here for a few days will help. He can brighten up any dark situation, and with my parents arguing and feeling a little rudderless without Rob, I'm ready to be brightened. And hopefully I can help my grandpa, too. I know he sometimes feels lonely living alone.

The rudderlessness—is that a word?—might not even come from the relationship ending in and of itself, but from losing the stability that a relationship provided.

Now? Everything's all loosey-goosey, willy-nilly. Anything could happen, and that feels terrifying.

Camilla taps her closed mouth before smiling. "Your grandpa, huh? Very interesting." She gives me a pointed look.

It dawns on me, and I gasp. "Cheesecake?"

Grandpa's cheesecakes are baked Christmas delights, with swirls of raspberry glaze and thick graham cracker crust enhanced with butter. Lots of it.

"What do you think, Aria? Should we go for it?"

"I'd love that. I could teach you how."

Camilla's mouth forms a tight line, and I know what that's about.

"Oh, the cheesecake curse."

"The cheesecake curse," Camilla echoes and then shivers. "It haunts me."

Camilla has golden baking fingers. She can bake anything—except cheesecake. Her grandfather tried to teach her, several times, without success. It boggles all of our minds. How is it possible that Camilla has a baking Achilles heel?

But she does.

Tears have been shed. A few times.

"Well, I can make them," I say. "I mean, it's only for a couple of months, right?"

She chews on her bottom lip, staring at me, before responding. "If you had the time, it would mean the world to me. Except, I don't want to tie you down. You're supposed to fly off and get your wings."

About that. Camilla, like the good friend that she is, has always said that when I'm ready to branch out, to get a job in a marketing or PR firm to help companies with their branding, that she would be my biggest cheerleader. That she'd hate to lose me, but she'd understand because she wants me to do what I love.

But that thought, especially with the family drama and the recent change in relationship status, has me feeling queasy.

"I'd never leave you during the busiest time of year, Camilla."

"If the right thing came along, you'd better." She shakes her head. "You just got the marketing degree. Besides, you're brilliant with branding work, and I can't afford you—what you're really worth."

I hold up a hand. "Let's cross that bridge when we come to it. As far as the cheesecake is concerned, consider it done. I'll make a couple tonight and bring them in for a taste test tomorrow."

"Shucks. You're my ride or die, you know that?" Camilla goes on her tip toes to ruffle the hair on the top of my head. But she's short and I'm tall, so she can't quite reach. She ends up scrubbing the top of my ear.

"Oh, I get by with a little help from my friends." I sing off-tune, but Camilla appreciates my low-key dance moves.

Later that night, I'm in my kitchen at home, still decorated in the cow-print décor of my youth, wishing grandpa were here already. It's going to be a long seven weeks until he comes.

"You're baking a cheesecake?" my mother asks when she comes in the kitchen for her nightly ritual of chamomile tea and saltine crackers.

"I bake!" I insist. "Sometimes." True, I don't usually need to. Camilla often fulfills my every baked good wish and more.

Mom tsks. "Don't use up all my sugar. I need it for my fudge." My mom makes Christmas fudge, and it's delectable—when we can snag some. Most of it goes to the neighbors.

"I bought my own sugar, Mom." I purchased all the ingredients I needed, and they weren't cheap. But I know Camilla has her suppliers where she can get things in bulk for less, if these turn out to be a viable option for Shorty's.

I turn on the food processor to crush more graham crackers for the second variety I'm making: a classic cherry version. When I'm done, I bring up the subject of the cheesecake again.

"I haven't made one in a while, so I wish Grandpa were here to make sure I'm doing it right. Camilla is thinking of serving this at Christmastime along with the shortbread."

"What do I smell?" my father asks as he enters the kitchen. He goes to the fridge to pull out the milk.

"She's baking cheesecakes, Dean. For Camilla."

My dad grunts as he moves to rummage in the cupboard. "I'll be your taste tester. I haven't had cheesecake since your grandpa was here last."

"No, you won't," Mom says. "It's too much sugar for this late at night." Her tone is both tired and sharp. She takes a sip of hot tea, then shunts a breath and sticks her tongue out. "Too hot."

Dad finds the small box of cinnamon candy and rips it open, inhaling the scent. "You enjoy making me miserable, I think," he says to Mom. He makes a clicking sound with his mouth before popping a candy into it. His tone is wry—tongue in cheek—but I know what's coming.

I try to direct the conversation to a better place. "I'm not going to slice the cheesecakes until tomorrow at the bakery, Dad. I need to show Camilla the presentation since she'll have them in the display case whole."

"So if you really want a slice of cheesecake, go to Shorty's." My mom says. "There. It's decided. And also?" Her voice goes up an octave, and I brace myself for the storm that's coming. "I do not enjoy making you miserable. It's miserable making you miserable."

Oh, boy.

He plunks down at the table and sets his glass down, hard. "Then why do it? Why can't you leave me alone?"

"I wish I could. You're the one who came in here while I was trying to unwind."

He pours the milk, raising the bottle high in the air and making the stream thin. He lowers the bottle just before the milk overflows. Mom rolls her eyes at his showing off.

"Guys. I thought you'd worked out a schedule," I say, mixing the graham cracker crumbs with the sugar and butter. If I can just get this last cheesecake done, I can hang out in my room while it bakes.

They'd decided one of them would take the earlier half hour to unwind in the kitchen with their signature nightly snack, and the other would go after. It was such a brilliant plan.

They both stare at me, as if they'd forgotten I was there.

My mother waves me away. "Did you know, Aria, that your father used to be so charming? Kind. Exciting and smart. Now? He likes to eat cinnamon candy, drink milk, and toss around insults." She shakes her head. "You'll understand when you're married," she says with a dull laugh. She takes a bite of cracker, so my dad jumps in with his own thoughts.

"Yes. She'll understand what *not* to do." He throws another candy in his mouth before taking a long swig of milk. Totally gross. But he's been doing it as long as I can remember. He has a hard time sleeping if he doesn't have his crazy snack.

I chide them lightly, since nothing else ever works, either. "You know, if you ever hope to have grandkids, you'd better start teaching us how to actually want this hot mess of an idea of marriage." I smile. Maybe if I say it in a joking tone I won't lose my temper, as I'm pretty sure they're fixing to do in this kitchen tonight.

The thing is, I *do* want to get married someday. I want to be a mom. It's just that when I think of it, I imagine my kids having to walk on eggshells and lying in their beds at night hearing the petty dialogue back and forth.

It's that thought right there, that hot mess, that makes me want to stay single for the next thousand years.

I manage to pour the creamy mixture into the crust, slide it into the oven, and disappear to my room before they start another round, something about a forgotten insurance payment.

My dad is right. I already understand what not to do.

Don't fall in love. Don't give my heart to anyone.

Chapter 4

Aria

"I just—wow! This is beautiful." Camilla steps to the counter and leans forward, inhaling the scent of the raspberry cheesecake.

I admire it, grinning. It's large, heavy, marbled with raspberry glaze and baked to what I hope is perfection.

"Try a slice," I say as I grab a knife and pie server from the drawer. Camilla reaches for a plate in the cupboards behind me. I carefully cut into it and raise it up with the pie server, one hand cupped around it like the Egyptian princess drawing Moses up out of the water.

I hand her the plate, and she first cuts off the tip of the slice and pushes it to the side then takes a bite. She chews thoughtfully.

"So?" I watch her, apprehension growing.

She rolls the flavors around in her mouth and swallows.

"It's like you're at a wine tasting," I say. "Come on. Tell me what you're thinking."

"Did you use lemon zest?" she asks.

"I did?" It's a question because what if that was wrong? I swear Grandpa added lemon zest to all of his cheesecakes, but maybe I used too much. Or not enough.

"That's brilliant. It's all brilliant, Aria." She cuts another piece away from hers with a fork and takes a slow bite.

"Really? You're not just saying that because you don't want to hurt my feelings?"

"Of course I'm being honest. I wouldn't beat around the bush with something like this."

I know she's right. She's always very serious these days about anything to do with her business.

"We'll sell it by the slice," she continues, "How many do you think you could make in a day?"

"I mean, as many as you need." I plate a slice for myself.

"Okay. I wish I could give you a hand, but you don't want the cheesecake curse to come anywhere near all this." She steeples her fingers like she's praying over it. "Aria. I'm very excited."

"Yay!" I squeal, take the fork from her fingers, and spear a small bit.

She shoots out a breath. "Not the tip! It's bad luck to eat the tip first. Save it for the end."

I shake my head. "You and your made-up rules." I use the fork to take off a bite from the remaining piece.

"It's not made up. It's a thing." At my laugh, Camilla raises her arms in the air. "Here's to world domination via baked goods!" she shouts.

That's right. And here's to helping Camilla get her business in the best possible shape before I strike out on my own.

If I can manage to strike out on my own.

The New Hedge Community Center is a hodge podge of humanity. It shares a building with the police department, the city administration offices, and the local DMV, so I'm turned around when I enter. Marjorie Clements and Liz Langer are up ahead, walking down the corridor, their heads together, talking. I know they're on the committee, so I jog to catch up with them. Liz teaches third grade at the elementary school and Marjorie works as a commissioner for the power plant. They're both long-time pillars of the community.

"Aria! So nice to see you," Liz says as I join them at the elevator.

"You two going to the festival meeting?" They're not wearing the Christmas blazers. Huh. I wasn't expecting them to just be in their regular clothes.

"Yes, are you?" Liz asks. "We hoped you'd come. We need your help now more than ever."

"I heard about the . . . concerns."

Marjorie places a hand on my arm. "Honey, you don't know the half of it."

Liz grows quiet, her brows jamming down over her eyes. We step into the elevator, my stomach turning at the thought that not all is right with the festival.

"Well, any pointers for me before we get there? I've never done this before."

"You'll catch on quickly," Marjorie assures. "It's a bit of a disadvantage to be joining in so late in the season because most things have already been decided and done. But we're happy to have someone your age to help us out. We have to leave a legacy for the future generations."

"What do you do for the committee?" I ask them as the elevator opens to a bright hallway. I follow them through the double doors. "I've never been up here before."

"No one has. Committee members only," Liz says. "Marjorie and I have done most everything over the years. It takes all year, you know. We've been meeting and planning this year's festival every week since January."

That is hardcore, I almost say. But we've reached the committee room, so the sentiment washes out before I can say it.

My senses are assaulted as I take in the room. It's a slightly worn, kitschy, overwhelmingly New Hedge version of Santa's workshop.

"What?" I stammer. "I've never seen anything like this." At least thirty people fill the room, all talking, all busy. The cacophony of colors and sounds assaults my eyes, but somehow there's an organized rhythm to it.

"We love having people join the committee." Liz clicks her tongue. "If only people knew what they were missing."

"Well, we love having the *right* people join the committee. We don't accept everyone who applies," Marjorie adds.

Overstuffed and aging recliners of all different shapes, sizes, and colors, complete with folding trays that hold laptops, phones, and charging stations line the room. Cozy Christmas quilts are thrown over the backs. The floors are flagstone, and three walls are covered with white boards and bulletin boards holding fabric swatches, print offs, drawings, and calendars. Costumes hang on a rack in the corner. It screams "my grandma's bridge club meets a think tank bursting with Christmas cheer."

"You made it!" Mara Franks rushes to me and wraps me in a hug. "We've got your station right here." She ushers me to the far corner around the semi-circle of recliners to one with cornflower blue upholstery.

I sit, still in a daze at this odd juxtaposition, enjoying the pillowy squishiness of the chair.

I don't even have time to get settled before *he* walks in.

Chapter 5

Theo

What is Aria Robinson doing at the Charles Dickens Christmas Festival meeting my boss forced me to go to?

And what is this place? A Christmas dreamland for adults ages fifty plus?

There is so much going on all around me, I don't know where to land my sights. There are at least thirty older model recliners, most of them seating Gen X-ers and Baby Boomers. I recognize many of them from work, the rec center, or my Saturday morning grocery shopping.

Liz Langer, the one who reached out to me this morning after Weatherby demanded I come, rushes up to me. She tugs on my hand. "Welcome! It's so nice to see fresh faces here!" She turns to an older gentleman seated on a black leather recliner. Her voice goes up several decimals as she leans toward his hearing-aid-assisted ear. "Isn't it nice to have fresh faces, Stewart?"

He nods, and I can only stare. I feel myself growing itchy where she's holding my hand. And come to think of it, my whole arm itches.

Which might be because I'm not a fan of Christmas. Even as a kid it brought up painful memories.

I love people. I probably couldn't be a very good attorney if I didn't. But right now I'm about as comfortable as a fish with a hook stabbed through its scaly lip.

Or mouth. Do fish have lips?

Liz drags me to a recliner right next to Aria, whose shock at seeing me has been rearranged to careful indifference.

"Here's your spot." She points to a brown suede recliner with a patchwork quilt in Christmas colors thrown over the arm. There's a stand perched off to the side where I'm assuming I can put my laptop, if I'd known to bring it.

This is all very weird. I don't know what Weatherby signed me up for.

When he told me I had to help with the Christmas Festival, I was thinking more along the lines of showing up to a couple of meetings, sitting in the back, signing up on a clipboard to help usher parking or cashier a few of the days, and bada bing bada boom, Weatherby will be happy, and I'll be good to go. One step closer to partner.

This? There is no hiding in the back.

Darrel Taylor doesn't move from his perch. He's reclined all the way, his forearms on the arm rests, his walrus mustache adding a venerable air, like he's the king of this unexpected castle.

"Welcome everyone. The meeting will now begin. We wish to thank Liz for arranging things with our newest committee members." He thrusts out a hand in our direction. "Will you please introduce yourselves?"

I glance at Aria, my mouth hanging open. Before I can gather my thoughts, she pipes up.

"Hi," she gives a little wave and a laugh, her back stiff. She hasn't reclined like everyone else has. "I'm Aria Robinson. I've lived here in New Hedge all my life and I recognize a lot of you here. I have to say, it was my childhood dream to work behind the scenes for the festival and I can't believe I'm here right now in this secret, special society."

The crowd laughs.

"I didn't know this was your secret dream," I whisper to her when it seems like she's done.

"You learn something new every day," she whispers back. "And this is Theo Carter," she tells the committee. "I have no idea what he's doing here, but—" She offers a stilted laugh.

"Neither do I," I say, hoping the burn in my cheeks subsides quickly. "I'm also happy to be here. I'm Theodore Vincent Carter, Esquire. I work with Weatherby and Knowles and just . . ." What more do I say? ". . . happy to contribute anyway I can."

I feel like I'm one of those professional athletes that are interviewed on television. *Just happy to be here, Bob. Go team!*

Aria mouths "Vincent?" She grins. "I had no idea."

"There's a lot you don't know about me," I whisper with a smile.

I turn back to Darrel Taylor, who nods.

"Thanks," Darrel says. "We appreciate you coming at the last minute. When things like this happen, we can only hope the controversy dies down quickly and doesn't detract from the important work we're doing." He sobers. "It's been a rough week. But we're glad you're here to help us dodge a very unfortunate bullet."

Unfortunate bullet? I glance at Aria, but she doesn't seem to understand either.

"Can you elaborate on the controversy?" I ask.

An itchiness settles over the room.

Marjorie Clements sinks into her own recliner near Darrel's. "Let's give you a little history lesson first. I'm finding your generation has little knowledge of what goes on to create the festival every year. They come to the festival and enjoy the booths as if they'd just appeared out of thin air. I think they think it's as magical as Santa Claus." She gestures in the air. "Pun intended."

Marjorie waits for the polite chuckles to subside. "This is a year-long project," she continues. "Most of us treat this like a part-time job. The festival has been running for thirty years. It's the most comprehensive, largest, most well-attended festival of its kind in the Intermountain West. When you begin to understand the amount of work involved, you understand why we've procured comfortable chairs for us over the years from Good Will. We deserve it."

A round of "hear, hear" ensues.

"Why don't we all go around the room and introduce ourselves," Darrel adds. "That way Theo and Aria can get to know everyone."

They do, and I think I recognize over half of the people. I've even represented a couple of them in minor family law cases.

"Where are Carl and Amanda?" Aria asks after everyone's been introduced.

Oh yeah. Carl and Amanda. The broadcast journalists who come in every year as the co-hosts of the festival. They're smooth and slick, doing press releases, hosting events, involving themselves in a lot of the PR. Their fame as local newscasters supposedly adds a nice touch. To me, I think the appeal is just that they're staples after this long.

"Well." Liz gives a bit of fake laughter. The air in the room shifts to an awkward unease. She turns to Aria and me. "Look guys. This is a sensitive subject and one that we really wish we didn't have to address." Her drying orange lipstick accentuates the cracks in her lips. "But we do. Especially because of what we're asking you to do." She pauses, as if gearing up to deliver a bomb. "Carl and Amanda are no longer the co-hosts of the festival."

Aria gasps and brings a hand to her mouth.

"It's not like they're dead," I offer in a whisper to her, surprised at her reaction. "At least, I don't think so." My head whips up to Liz.

"Dead? Carl and Amanda?" Marjorie asks. "Oh no. They're very much alive."

"We only wish they were dead." A man's voice deadpans behind me.

"Now, Sheldon. That's not nice of you to say," Marjorie says.

"What? We're all thinking it, right?" he shoots back.

A low murmur snakes its way around the room.

Liz clears her throat. "Regardless of our personal opinions about their actions, we have a job to do. The festival starts in less than a month. We've got to do all we can to nip any ill effects from Carl and Amanda's choices in the bud. We've got to keep our focus on the festival itself."

"And wring their spray-tanned necks later?" Now it's a woman's voice, and those sitting next to her laugh.

Liz pulls the lever on her rocker recliner with such force she shoots up and out of it with impressive speed. "We have the dignity of the festival to think of. We won't be reduced to a scandalous memory." Her pointer finger punctuates her words. "We *will* see this through. Without mocking or indulgences." Her eyes, large and round, twitch, unblinking, as she stares everyone down.

Darrel clears his throat. "Look. Guys." His gaze goes between Aria and me. "Basically, Carl and Amanda have been ousted because the charity they formed, as an arm of the festival, Shoes and Dues, turned out to not be so charitable."

The reedy voice of Stewart, the hard of hearing one, has more vinegar than I could have predicted. "They told everyone the money goes to kids' shoes and to help pay for their involvement in the arts and sports programs. Well, they lied. They've kept most of that money for themselves for years."

"Yeah, Shoes and Dues?" a woman two chairs down from me adds. "More like Poo Poos."

Another voice pipes up. "Carl and Amanda don't have a clue!"

"I hope they get the flu!"

I can't stop a snigger at the impromptu rhymes.

"Okay, okay," Liz says, holding out her arms. "That's enough, everybody. It is a bit of a trainwreck, though," she says to Aria and me. "Since word got out two days ago, we've been fielding complaints. Several vendors have pulled their booths from the festival and sponsors are withdrawing. This is serious. It feels like there are people out there grouping us all together—like they're fixing to cancel culture us! We are not Carl and Amanda and their sorry excuse for a charity!"

"It would be a shame to have the festival negatively affected by this," I agree.

"It's not okay for everyone to assume the festival had anything to do with that," Aria says.

"Which is why it's all-hands-on-deck," Marjorie joins Liz. "Our community has to band together. If the festival—" she swallows, and her bottom lip trembles, "—can't overcome the negative press, the outrage—well, we have to do all we can to make sure the festival goes on."

"We've been in touch with Santa's Helpers," Darrel says. "A charity that's near and dear to many people around here. Partnering with them instead could do a lot for our public image."

Liz steps closer to our recliners. "Aria, we've loved the graphic design and branding work you've done for us. We appreciate you volunteering your talents and precious time to help turn this around. I know with your skills we can spin this back in our favor. And your age is a bonus too. If you couldn't tell, we're all getting on in age."

"Did she say we're getting on in age?" Stewart asks the person next to him. When they nod, he grumbles, "Ah, speak for yourself!"

Darrel's moustache twitches. "We wanted to hand the reins over to someone younger."

Aria looks confused.

Darrel turns to me. "And Mr. Carter? You were recommended by Allen Weatherby as someone who can keep an eye on things, to head off any potential legal dangers we might be getting in as a result of Carl and Amanda's, uh, poor decisions." He frowns and shakes his head.

"And look at you!" Now Liz is beaming. "Don't they look gorgeous together?" There are murmurs of agreement. "I think our decision is perfect. With your professionalism, you can make the whole area forget all about the scandal."

"Yeah, everyone will be saying 'Carl and Amanda who?'" Marjorie adds.

"I don't understand," Aria says, sitting forward in her chair.

"You two are the new Carl and Amanda!" Liz announces. "The faces of the festival!"

Chapter 6

Aria

I shoot out of my chair at Liz's announcement, except I don't need the lever to propel me. The shock is enough to get me going. They want *me* to host the festival?

Well, co-host, technically. With Theo.

"You okay?" Liz asks. She's smiling and her voice is gentle, but there's a slight crack in her façade, a wobble to her perky exterior.

"Yeah, are you okay, Aria?" Theo asks.

I turn to Theo. He's smiling playfully, amused at my surprise. He's unfairly handsome, with his casual, plaid button-down shirt and fitted khakis. His sneakers are nice, and on anyone else, they'd seem juvenile, like he's a punk teen. But somehow, it works for him. The outfit and shoes fit his young-professional vibe.

I only shake my head at Liz and Marjorie. Which turns into a nod. "Yeah. Yes. That sounds . . . fantastic. I can do that."

The blazer. The Christmas blazer with the candy canes and holly and those weird little jacks-in-the-box. I lick my lips. I want this. Can I actually do this? Doubt floods my entire being, nearly causing me to stumble.

"Except, are you sure?" I ask. "I mean, I'm not a journalist like Carl and Amanda." I give a sideways glance at Theo, unsure of what he's thinking. "We're not journalists at all."

Liz makes a *tut-tut* sound. "We don't want journalists. We need to freshen things up. We need a younger vibe now. Aria and Theo, you're perfect for the job."

Theo chuckles, running his fingertips over his barely-there beard. "And what exactly does this entail?"

Marjorie gives a satisfied nod, as if to say, *now we're getting somewhere*. "Glad you asked. We need to do a photo shoot ASAP. We're in the process of removing everything that has Carl and Amanda's likenesses on it and so we'll be working to replace those. You'll host events. We'll do all the planning and prep. You get to show up and greet everyone and make announcements. We can send you film from previous years to give you an idea."

"Film?" It's a reminder that I'll be the center of attention. I'm not an extreme extrovert like Camilla, but I might be able to handle this. I can swallow my pride for this gig. Plus, it could help my career. Any publicity I would get as the face of the festival could help me find potential branding clients.

"And we'll need to fit you for your Christmas blazers and your Dickensian costumes," Liz says.

"Blazers," I breathe.

At the same time, Theo says, "Costumes?"

Being co-host of the most well-known festival around would look killer on a resume. But more than that, if I can get people to understand that the festival is not Carl and Amanda and their fake charity, then it will be worth the time commitment. I can stand being in the spotlight if it means saving the festival.

And, come on. I'll get a blazer.

Liz chuckles. "This is the Charles Dickens Christmas Festival, Theo. It's an historic treasure. And as the face of the festival, when you're not wearing the blazer, you'll be wearing your fair share of period clothing to look the part."

Theo's jaw is set tight.

Who's all easy breezy now, huh?

"We don't mind the costume part." I glance at Theo, an attempt to encourage him along. "And I'll be thrilled to wear the blazer."

Theo shoots out a breath and scratches at the back of his neck.

"I'll email over a schedule of everything that's going on. Everything that we'll need you to come to," Marjorie says. Her voice is calm and soft. "Just fittings, the photo shoot, and a few events. Oh, and there's the dinner."

"Dinner?" Theo is pacing now, his arms crossed severely over his chest, his hands balled in fists.

Darrel clears his throat. "The beginning of December, Carl and Amanda host a big dinner for us and all the VIPs in the area. Sort of a thank you to the sponsors and what not. That's the only thing you'll have to plan ahead. Carl and Amanda had it catered. The rest of us are pretty busy the week before the festival starts, so we can't do it. I guess it's your way of saying thanks to all involved."

"Let me get this straight," Theo says. He's stopped pacing and his face has gone a little pale. "We plan and host a dinner to thank you for everything you've done?"

I reach out a hand to Theo. "It's tradition. It's to show gratitude to everyone, not just the committee. We'll get it all figured out. And maybe we can reach out to Carl and Amanda to see what they've gotten done on it so far." I shrug. "Maybe we won't need to do much."

"They—" Liz frowns. "I think it would be best if we severed all ties with them now. We have their electronic files. We'll send them to you. No need to contact them." Her voice is rushed, panicked.

"Has any legal recourse been started?" Theo asks. "Is anyone suing Carl and Amanda?"

A hush settles over the room. "Suing?" Marjorie's voice cracks. "I certainly hope not. Let's move forward with the festival. If we can partner with Santa's Helpers, we can show the general public that we're sorry about the past decisions of the former co-hosts, and we're doing all we can to make things right." She chews on her bottom lip.

Liz places a hand on Theo's shoulder. "You might be asked about this in interviews, but perhaps the only acceptable answer to those questions is 'no comment,' or 'next question.'"

"That's something we can discuss," he says. "It would be good to have a plan of what to say. Some talking points."

I see a side of Theo I've never seen before. He looks perplexed. Upset, even.

But it doesn't last. "This is a big commitment." Theo flashes a winning, flirty smile at Marjorie and Liz. "Do you mind if Aria and I take a moment to discuss?"

"Oh, of course we don't mind. We'll get started with other items of business while you two have a little chat." Liz walks past us and leads us into a narrow hallway. "That room on the left is empty. Feel free to talk in there." She smiles widely at us, her brows climbing up her face. "And please understand, we and the whole city of New Hedge thank you for your sacrifices to the cause. I just know your efforts are going to bring in so much cash for gifts for the kids."

She shuffles us inside and then closes the door with a bang.

"She had to bring up the kids, huh? That's a little unfair." Theo slings his long body into one of the chairs at the small table.

I set my bag down on the table and slowly sink into the opposite chair, guarded. "This feels like an interrogation room."

"I wonder if they brought Carl and Amanda in here to question them." Theo's grin is wide.

"I think that law was a solid career choice for you," I say with a laugh. "Let's just get this over with. What are we going to do?"

"First of all, I'm going to give Weatherby a piece of my mind."

"No, you're not. He holds your future in his hands."

"That's painfully true," Theo concedes. "And he didn't exactly give me a choice. He said his wife is concerned—'in a tizzy' were his exact words—that the festival might not happen this year because of Carl and Amanda. He promised her he'd get me involved. He told me I need to 'save the festival' and if I do, I'll get the Dahlen account."

"What's the Dahlen account?"

"It's a big deal. The mother lode." He nods slowly. "High profile and a lot of billable hours, but it's also the biggest opportunity I've had yet. It's what I've been waiting for."

"I hope you get it."

"Thanks. And I hope we can save the festival, whatever that means."

"Did he give you any ideas on how he expected you to save it?" The thought of the festival ceasing to exist this year lights a fire in my belly.

"No. I thought he was being dramatic. He didn't tell me much about it." He drums his fingers on the table.

The man can't hold still. Why do I find that kind of cute? He must notice my vague smile in his direction because he looks like he's now fighting back a smile. So many smiles.

"I have a confession to make," he says, his eyes narrowing in my direction, like he doesn't want to admit whatever he's about to say.

"Oh no."

"I don't like Christmas. I feel like you should know that upfront."

My mouth goes wide. "Are you serious right now?"

He lifts a shoulder. "It's not a crime. I'm just not a fan."

"In New Hedge, that's definitely a crime, Theo. How can you not like Christmas? That's like saying, I really don't like breathing, or eating."

His mouth bunches up. "No reason, really. My mom and my stepfather, Odin, tried to make it fun for Jesse and me when we were little. But it's not my favorite."

There's more to this. That much is clear. But I'm not going to press him on it. Maybe when he was a kid, he broke his arm on Christmas Day. Or maybe his great-uncle choked on some peanut brittle and died. Whatever it was, I'm going to have to wait to find out.

I change the subject. "I'm upset about Carl and Amanda." I shift in my chair.

His jaw grates to one side. "Me, too. I can't tolerate that level of self-serving deception."

"Is that why you became an attorney?" I reach over and fluff the top of his hair. Not sure why . . . "To right the wrongs of society?"

"Something like that." He hesitates. "And so I can buy BMWs." He places a hand over his heart.

Dramatic little pill.

"So, are we doing this?" I ask. "Because as I see it, you don't have a choice. And I could say no, but the festival's an institution that I'd hate to see go away." Hate is an understatement. I'd go ballistic on anyone who jeopardizes this piece of heaven. "Carl and Amanda better hope I never run into them in a dark alley."

He leans back in his chair, lacing his fingers together behind his head. "I'd like to see that, actually."

I narrow my gaze at him. "Whatever. But I do have some concerns."

"You don't want to work with me." He leans forward and rests his elbows on the table.

I lean back. Wow. Spot on. "Like I said, I have concerns."

He shakes his head slowly. "Are you going to tell me what they are? No sense being indirect."

"Well, we're opposites in most ways. And we don't exactly get along."

His smile is rakish. "I can put aside our differences for the sake of the festival and my career. Can you?"

My mouth drops open. "Of course, I *can*. It's just going to be difficult."

"I get it. We're opposites." He leans forward even more. "Being around you doesn't worry me." His smile has an undercurrent of sadness. "But the costumes? Please. Kill me now."

"You just don't want to dress up because it might cramp your style with the ladies."

This hits a nerve. His posture goes stiff, and he stares at me. We haven't ever discussed the incident at the bakeshop the day after Camilla and Jesse's wedding, where, after my words about his other women, his girlfriend, or whatever she was, sprayed him with water and stormed out. For all I know, she broke up with him.

But we've never talked about it. And for the record, I didn't cause any of that. It was his two-timing, or three-timing ways, as it were, that caused his downfall. Maybe the woman would even like to thank me for shedding light on the matter.

"I'm not concerned about the ladies." His face grows sober.

"Yeah right." I roll my eyes so hard, there's a sharp flash of pain behind them. Ouch.

"I'm not," he insists.

"Why? Because even a stupid costume won't detract from your beauty?" I ask him.

He laughs and holds up his palms. "You said it. Not me."

I shake my head. "Nope. I didn't mean—"

"I'm starting to care less about what women, what others in general, think of me, or at least, I'm trying to." He looks uncomfortable in his own skin, and he fidgets with his shirt sleeves, pushing them up his arms and then back down again. "So it's not about that. I just want to do well at the firm. I want to help my clients. And if being poster boy for the festival will be a means to that end, then so be it."

I shrug. "You're really not concerned about the two of us working together?"

He studies me carefully, his knee bobbing up and down. "I've never not liked you, Aria. I don't know why you think that."

I want to bring up the incident in the bakeshop all those months ago, but I can't seem to form the words.

"Okay. But in light of your previous actions, flirting with me is out of the question. And we have to both be all in. No slacking. No leaving the other person to do all the work."

"That's not like me. I don't slack off."

His casual, young vibe aside, Camilla and Jesse have mentioned that as far as his career is concerned, Theo is as committed and hardworking as they come.

"And can we treat each other professionally?" I raise a brow. By that, I mostly mean, can *he* treat *me* professionally?

"You have a boyfriend. Ever since I've found that out, I've respected those boundaries and will continue to do so."

Oh. About that . . . But I'm not ready to tell him Rob and I broke up. The more distance he believes we need, the safer this situation will be.

"Okay, thanks. And I'll try my best to be civil. For the sake of the festival."

"And what's in it for you?" he asks, shrugging. "Is this a power thing?"

I sigh. "Theo. They're in a bind, and in some ways, it would be a good networking opportunity for me as I branch out."

"Branch out? You fixing to leave Camilla's bakeshop?"

No. We are not going there. I'm not going to be talking about my personal future plans with Theo.

I hold up a hand. "That's neither here nor there. The festival was an important part of my childhood. And we live in New Hedge. It's sorta the town's thing, to help each other out, don't you think?"

"Agreed. We can fake it. We can pretend we're best buddies."

"You maybe can." I offer a bleak smile and shake my head. "I can't."

"Oh, are you morally incapable of lying?"

"No. Yes." I slump in my chair and rest my head in my hands. "Talking to you hurts. We're going in circles and it's exhausting."

"The way I see it, I don't really have a choice. My boss is asking me to do this, and I can't say no. But you can. How about I tell them yes and that you'll need to be reassigned. They can find another leading lady for me." He stands from the table as if that settles it.

But it doesn't. This is an amazing opportunity, and I'm not going to let him ruin it for me. "Theo. Let's just agree to do this and not kill each other in the process, okay?"

A slow smile smirks across his face as he stands in front of me. "I can be civil. Can you?"

I step towards him, my gaze darting around his face, taking in his blue-eyed, dark-haired presence. "Oh, I'll be civil. I'll kill you with civility."

"It's decided then." He holds out his hand for me to shake, and I almost brush past him. I don't need a dorky handshake. I need to get back into the committee room and get this party started.

But at the last minute, I whirl around and reluctantly take his hand. It's larger than I expected it to be. And the shake is firm, like he's confident, but not arrogant.

The man has nice, manly man hands.

"Here's to surviving the next few weeks," I say.

He grins, his eyes crinkling at the corners. "Like Marjorie says, it's Christmas time. Let's try to have some fun."

Fun? We'll see.

Chapter 7

Theo

I'm not prepared for what's staring back at me in the full-length mirror in the photography studio dressing room. I'm in a charcoal-colored suit from the mid-1800s. I think the costumer called it a frock coat? Whatever it is, I've been transformed, but it's not like I'm suddenly Theo Carter 2.0, bigger, better, faster.

I'm Theo Carter .02, a clown in this out-of-place suit.

I sigh then try to shift my scowl into something that Charles Dickens would do. What did he even look like? Was he smiley and jolly? Or more like Scrooge?

I personally feel like Scrooge. I don't let things get me down eleven months of the year. But my own personal version of torture is the mall at Christmastime. All those holiday commercials trying to tug at our heartstrings with families coming together—yeah right. And the Christmas lights? They hurt my eyes and give me a headache.

Doesn't matter. I'm doing this to promote—and save—the festival, which in turn appeases Weatherby, which in turn will give me the Dahlen case. Which betters the chances I'll make partner. That I get to spend time with Aria is a very fortunate bonus, not that she sees it as such.

We've already gotten our pictures taken in those terrible Christmas blazers, and now we've traveled back in time to old London.

There's a brisk knock and then Liz bursts into the room. She clutches her neck. "What a dapper man about town you are!"

I offer a chuckle, but I'm nervous. I've sort of milked my looks, okay? I learned from an early age how to do that.

Healthy? No. Effective? Sometimes.

But now? I don't know what to think. I'm like an old-fashioned penguin. I feel naked, which is saying something since I'm clearly overdressed.

I feel vulnerable.

And I don't do vulnerable.

Liz grasps my arm. "Aria's nearly ready. You two are going to sell tickets, I tell you what!" She drags me out of the dressing room, down the hall, and into the portrait studio, which is set up to look like a snowy mid-nineteenth century London street.

I'm fussed over, so many older women poking at my suit, smoothing it out, and arguing over whether or not I should be holding a hat under my arm for the photos.

"We ready to start?" I ask the growing crowd. I smile about it—might as well embrace it—but all I can think about is how I need some billable hours at the firm. And this? There are no billable hours happening. I'm not making a dime right now.

Which is tough. But I have to remember it's an investment into my future.

"Such a handsome brow," one of the women says.

"Reminds me of Superman in that movie, *Somewhere in Time.*"

"That actor's name was Christopher Reeve, and it took place about sixty years after this time period," Marjorie scolds.

I start to laugh, but that's when Aria comes into view. My breath hitches. She's standing in the corner of the room wearing a dark-red velvet ball gown.

I'm by her side before I know it. Her long, dark hair is pinned up and her dress is off the shoulder, her neckline bare. I've never noticed the shell shape of her ears before. And her warm, tan skin and luminous eyes are magnets pulling me to her. I can't look away.

"You look—" I stop myself. Aria's not like other women who respond to compliments. She may or may not appreciate me gushing over her. But I can't help it. She's breathtaking. If I was drawn to her before, that was nothing compared to what's going on now.

I clear my throat. "You look enchanting." I offer a little bow that fits the esthetic of the photoshoot. Maybe if I get into the part we can be done sooner.

"As do you, kind sir," she says lifting a gloved hand.

I take it and press my lips to her fingers. She sears me with a look, but then takes in a deep breath.

"Curse the man, or whoever it was who dictated women's fashion back then." She places both hands on her waist. "Corsets." She breathes out.

Her waist is sculpted, the fabric of her dress pleats circling and cinching her in tightly. "I'm sure it's torture to wear. But you look—"

"Speechless again?" She laughs, and the ringlets framing her face bounce from side to side. This look isn't supposed to work. It's old-fashioned with a capital *O*. On anyone else, it's comical. A costume.

On Aria? It's unbelievably beautiful.

"Okay, you two. Let's get started," the photographer's assistant says.

We pose next to a brick backdrop dusted with fake snow. I'm asked to place my hand on her back, and I breathe in her strawberry scent.

"You're both tall, so you pull off this style incredibly well," the photographer says from behind the camera.

"They're such a beautiful couple," says Liz with a sigh.

A couple? She remembers this is only for promotional purposes, right? Not that I would mind exploring couple-like opportunities with Aria. She excites me endlessly. But she's more of a serious relationship kind of person. And I am not.

Still, if she'd go on one official date with me . . .

"Angle your head to look at him, Aria," the photographer commands as the assistant reaches in for a quick adjustment of her hair.

Aria turns her head, and we lock gazes. The air is sucked out of me, and I struggle not to let it show. There's a frisson between us, pulling me to her, drinking in everything that she is. Her faint dusting of cinnamon freckles across her nose about does me in. Desire shifts through me, swift and strong.

"It's snowing!" Liz says, wiping her shoes off on the mat when she comes into the room. She flicks the top of her head and beads of moisture fling off in all directions. "Let's step outside and get some authentic snow, shall we?"

The whole party moves out through the double doors and onto a grassy area next door. It's the first snow of the season and I have to admit, it's magical, even if it's just a skiff.

Aria bends down, gathers a tiny snowball in both hands, and lifts it to my face. "If we weren't in a photo shoot right now, I'd plaster you with this." Her eyes are daring.

"If we weren't in a photo shoot, I'd dump you in a snowbank."

"There aren't any snowbanks. There's barely any accumulation," she insists.

"I can be patient." And I can. Aria might dislike me; she might think she knows me. But I can wait for her to come around, as difficult as it may be.

The tiny, heavy beads of snow soon grow into larger, fluffy flakes, falling slowly all around us, and the photographer's excited about how the shots look. He has us pose so that Aria is facing away from me, her back against my front. My hands go around her waist, and even through the ridiculous torture device that is the corset, I can feel her strength, the smoothness of her body. Her clean, berry scent is in my nose, tripping me up, setting me up for disappointment.

She shivers.

"Are you cold?" I whisper.

Her only response is a fluttering of her eyelashes before she looks again at the camera.

"Can we get a blanket for her?" I ask the assistant.

Within moments, the assistant places a white, woolen shawl over her shoulders.

"Thank you." Aria fusses with the shawl, focusing on it instead of me.

Is she flustered?

"Okay, we've gotten a lot of serious expressions." The photographer says. He's looking at us like he knows. Like he can see what's happening between us. "Now, let's mix it up. Let's have some fun."

Aria frowns and looks at me doubtfully. It's a challenge, even if she's not meaning it to be.

"You don't think I can make you laugh?" I ask. "Me? Class clown extraordinaire?"

She folds her arms across the vee in her dress at the waist. "I'm not saying it's impossible, but . . ."

I do a deep knee bend and then spin around. "You're not the only one who took dance." I tell her as I whip my body around in a pirouette of sorts. I don't stick the landing very well, but I don't have to. She looks impressed and her head tips back in a laugh.

"How did you know I took dance? And when did you take it?"

"I know because I can tell just by looking at you. And, Camilla mentioned it once." I do another pirouette, muscle memory taking over. "I had a phase in fourth grade. Wanted to do hip-hop, but my instructor made me also do some ballet because he said it would help my hip-hop skills."

It was a short phase. My mom was still single at that time. After my father ruined her reputation as an attorney, as well as his own, he left us. And because of all that happened, she systematically lost all her clients in the aftermath of my dad's actions. She was so heartbroken, her hopes so ruined, that she decided to leave the law profession altogether. Which is why she couldn't afford lessons for very long.

"I also learned this," I tell her as I kick my leg out to the side, as far as I can, and then jump, shooting my bottom leg up to meet the one in the air. It's a hitch kick. Probably the best one that I've ever done. And Aria's head goes back in a laugh, her hand on her chest, radiant joy on her face.

It's the most compelling, gorgeous thing I've ever seen.

<h1 style="text-align:center">Chapter 8</h1>

Aria

I park behind the bakeshop, and, completely unbidden, my thoughts turn to Theo. There was trouble in the vibe he carried into the photo shoot. Typical Theo, confident with a dash of uncertainty—a vulnerability I've never seen from him before.

He would have fit quite nicely into that era, those clothes working well on his frame. And the way it felt to be pressed up against him for the photos as I was wearing that low-cut dress with those ridiculous ringlets in my hair?

I thought I'd be embarrassed. I thought I'd feel silly.

But because of the way he looked at me, I felt . . . strong.

In my whole life, I don't think I've ever been looked at like that. And, in response, I felt . . . things. Things that were totally against my will.

Which is completely unacceptable.

I force him out of my mind as I reach the back door of the bakeshop. The snow from yesterday didn't stick, but there are still some fingerlings of frost on the windows. Since Shorty's is open later now, I don't come in until the morning's warmed up a little. Danene still comes in early to make all the bread. But Camilla and me? We get the luxurious time of nine a.m.

Except, I've already been up a couple of hours, trying to get some work done for the festival—my skin tingles with pride at that thought. I've been compiling some graphics for their website in an attempt at a total rebrand. We have to separate ourselves from the old Carl-and-Amanda days.

Doesn't mean I didn't love sliding on the classic Christmas blazer for the first time. It fit me like a glove, like I somehow *knew* it would. We might be trying to update the festival, but I'll never advocate for getting rid of the blazers. Never.

Camilla grins from ear to ear when I walk into Shorty's industrial, recently remodeled kitchen. "So? How was dressing up yesterday?"

"Have you ever had to wear a corset?"

She washes her hands. "I have. Not that I'd want to again. There's a reason why our Victorian dresses for the festival have been more the third-class variety. Ain't nobody got time for corsets!"

"I don't have time or energy for them, but I had to wear one yesterday and I about died," I tell her, pulling up a selfie I took in the mirror in the photo studio dressing room.

She screams and her mouth drops open. "You look—" She stops herself and shakes her head, a grin taking over her expression.

"You sound like Theo yesterday." I say with a snort. "Speechless."

Part of me sort of loved that he liked what he saw. I don't care what he thinks of me—far from it. But my petty, immature self likes that he thought I looked pretty in that red velvet.

"Enchanting," as he called it. Which is satisfying in some odd way. It shouldn't be. Theo's a womanizer—attracted to anything that moves.

The whole thing was interesting—the way his arm felt around me as we posed for the camera. Theo's touch was a bowl of cream for a half-starved kitten.

"You look hot," Camilla says, donning her hair net and head band. "I'm not surprised Theo was speechless."

Her teasing smile makes me groan.

I slide my phone in my pocket and turn on the hot water at the sink. "Not like that. I think we were both surprised that our clothing actually looked okay. I don't know what the committee is going to do with all those photos. I feel like they own us." I shake my head. "Speaking of the committee, you would not believe their complex underworld. Camilla, it's like a whole, secret society. "

Her eyebrows shoot up to her hairnet. "I love a good conspiracy theory. Is Liz Langer a witch in real life?"

I laugh. "No. And I didn't get the sense there are conspiracies going on, but there is the scandal they hope disappears. And they are hardcore. This festival is their life, which I sort of love."

"I always knew something about Carl and Amanda was off."

"I'm not supposed to say anything." I hedge, knowing I'm going to anyway. It's Camilla.

I dry my hands with a paper towel and tell her the latest, that Shoes and Dues is being investigated by the police department. I explain that, despite the overall tone of smarminess Carl and Amanda exuded as they kept such a large percentage of the donations, they might not have actually broken the law.

"Their charity's 401C documents state clearly that Carl and Amanda will get such a high percentage of the donations to distribute how they see fit, which protects them."

"Still. It's not okay that they saw fit to pad their own wallets without being upfront about what they were doing," Camilla says.

"Yes." I tie my apron snugly around my middle. "And the festival is what New Hedge is known for, so Carl and Amanda's actions reflect poorly on the whole thing," I say. I readjust my hair net and bright pink and orange head wrap. "I'm still wondering about how this whole co-host thing works. We're the face of the festival this year."

"Let me know how I can help. And if you need to take time off . . ."

She tapers her words and I know what she's thinking, that this is the busiest time of year for Shorty's Bakeshop. We not only have a lot to do to get ready for our own booth at the festival, but it's shortbread season. With cheesecakes to make, my busyness is going to be difficult for her.

Camilla needs to get used to seeing less of me anyway, and that has nothing to do with Shorty's busy time of year.

But I'm not going to think about that huge sweeping change right now.

"There will be times I can't be at Shorty's booth specifically," I say.

"It's okay." Camilla raises her chin. "We'll make it work. Maybe Danene will come help."

"Except she swore she'd never wear one of those dresses. I was thinking Elijah could help out? He said he wants more hours."

"That kid would look adorable as Tiny Tim," Camilla says.

"Tiny Tim? Elijah's eighteen and pushing six feet tall."

"True. But I kind of feel protective of him like I would Tiny Tim. Don't you?"

I nod. He's almost like a little brother to me.

I turn to log onto the register and finish other opening preparations. Camilla and I do our odd opening dance, the same one we've done every morning since she took over her deceased grandfather's shop. It's part duck with a high school cheer squad tone and I feel like an idiot doing it. But it's Camilla's thing, the thing that gets her revved up for the day. And it's only a few seconds long. I can handle it.

We work into the afternoon, and I only wonder a couple of times if Theo's next door at the firm.

That's good. I can't allow my mind to get derailed just because I'm a little lonely around Christmas time or because of everyone fussing over us being a "cute couple." I can't get derailed by memories of the intimacy of the photo shoot.

There's a lull before the storage unit customer crowd starts coming in around four o'clock, so I work on my branding portfolio and start some cheesecakes, too. I get out the supplies and measure, whip, beat, and bake my way to five large cheesecakes in only about an hour. It's a pretty fast and easy process for what I hope will be a profitable source of income for the shop. Anything that I can do to help.

I'm technically off at five, and even though we still have a steady stream of customers, the food prep is long over, and Camilla can handle it on her own. As I step outside, the sidewalk is dry. That first snowfall didn't last long. I climb in my car and start up the engine.

As I round the back alley and drive out onto the main road, I realize I didn't check to see if Theo's BMW was parked in our bakeshop spots. But my pride at avoiding Theo is cut short as I notice the freeway's electronic billboard just down the way.

"It's me!" I scream.

I behold the digital sign in shock.

"The Charles Dickens Christmas Festival" is in bright gold, serif letters, an overlay on a photo of Theo and me. I've got my head thrown back in laughter, my hand at my throat. Theo's cleared the ground by several feet. I hadn't realized he'd hitch kicked so high, although I wouldn't put it past the committee to photo shop that a little. He's grinning from ear to ear, and he looks so free, so happy.

He's usually happy and carefree, but sometimes I wonder if it's more of a shield than reality. Still, in that photo, as he's jumping to impress me, to make me laugh, he looks downright giddy. Perfect for the part.

I'm relieved the committee didn't choose one of the more intimate photos, where I'm in Theo's arms.

My phone rings, and I answer it as I merge onto the freeway.

"Aria," my father says, his tone serious. "It's about your grandfather."

Chapter 9

Theo

It's been a couple of days since the photo shoot, and I still have Aria on the brain.

Weatherby asks me to go over to our new building and provide him a status update on the renovator's progress. I don't mind. No, these aren't billable hours, which is unfortunate for my drive to gain all the dollar bills. But it's fine because I'll stop into Shorty's, see how Aria's doing, and hopefully get myself a baked good or two while I'm at it.

The bell over the door chimes as I come in. There's a good feeling in the air when that happens, like we're in some Norman Rockwell painting or on the set of a cheesy family sitcom—when times were decent and relatively stress-free.

Or maybe that's just me remembering my childhood that wasn't at all stress-free, but in which I watched reruns of old shows like

Family Matters because my mom couldn't afford cable. It was the only interesting thing on our four local channels.

I don't know. Being in Shorty's feels nice, until Aria eyes me cautiously before I've even reached the counter.

It's the status quo, the default we've fallen into since our awkward first meeting. If I had any illusions that things would be different now that we're co-hosts of the festival—and since our photo shoot yesterday—I guess I was wrong.

"Milady," I say, tipping my imaginary hat. I won't let her get me down, at least not outwardly. Might as well play up my role as her dashing leading man.

"Hey," she says before flicking her eyes to her laptop screen. I step to the side and catch a glimpse of an intricate graphic of a heavily wooded, snowy scene.

"That's cool. Is it for the festival?"

Aria nods, her eyes trained on the screen. "I'm creating graphics for the committee. They're asking all of us volunteer designers to do all we can to totally rebrand the festival. Gotta help save it, you know?"

"Aria's so good at design that she needs to branch out. Get a real job," Camilla says with a laugh, carrying a metal cake preserver through the swinging kitchen door.

"I have a real job. Right here."

"Just don't ever think I'm trying to hold you back from your dreams. I want you to stay forever. But if you did, I'd feel responsible for you being stifled. You're destined for greatness at a big-time firm."

I take in Aria and nod my head enthusiastically. "You're reinventing yourself all over the place. That's exciting."

When she only twists her mouth to one side, Camilla chimes in. "I'm hoping doing the festival rebrand will get her thinking outside the box." She sets the cake stand on the counter and opens her mint green display case.

"Are you serving cheesecake now?" I ask Camilla.

"Aria, get him a complimentary slice." Camilla leaves the case door open and moves to return to the kitchen. She looks back before she disappears. "You know the rule, though, Theo."

"Glad to see Camilla has you under some semblance of order." Aria says, her lips toying with a smile.

"Camilla's rule, in case you don't know, involves me promising to spread the word if the samples she gives me are good," I tell her.

"And do you comply?"

"Every time." I say, and I mean it. I think my friends, coworkers, and clients are probably tired of hearing about the bakery's many dope products, but I don't care. I'll proselytize all day long.

She sighs, eyes me warily again, and then reaches for a plate and the pie server in the glass case. She draws out a slice of the cherry marbled cheesecake, slides it on the plate, and gathers a paper napkin and plastic fork. "Would you like anything else?" she asks, her eyes flicking to the laptop before returning to mine.

"I'm sure you want to get back to what you were doing. But did you see our billboard?"

Two triangles of pink overtake her upper cheeks. "I did. I think they photoshopped your hitch kick."

"What? No. I got that high."

She giggles. "You sure, Theo?"

"Positive. But we can ask Liz to be sure. Besides, it doesn't bother me either way. It's an awesome photo. A lot of people think so."

"Who? Like your mom? Jesse? All your ladies on the side?"

Is she fishing for info on my dating life again? "I don't have any ladies on the side." I raise my chin in the air. "I've turned over a new leaf."

She snorts a laugh. "That's good to hear."

"Is it?"

She waves me away. I don't think she believes me, but I'm not going to press the issue. The truth is, I haven't been on a date in months, not since Elisha dumped me after Aria told her the truth about my bringing another woman to my brother's wedding.

I sober as I remember. I shouldn't have asked Gelsey to the wedding. It was a rash, last-minute decision that I regretted the minute I'd done it. I didn't want to ask Elisha because we hadn't reached the "attend a family wedding" stage in our relationship. Bringing a woman you're dating to your brother's wedding is a big deal, and I wasn't about to turn up stag. And Gelsey's an old friend, who happens to be a former model with a very open, noncommittal public-display-of-affection policy that I had a hard time reining in.

It meant nothing, to Gelsey or to me. Still, it was immature and unfair to Elisha, and she had every right to dump me.

But why am I thinking of all this right now? Because it was Aria, clearly bothered by my dating patterns, that woke me up. If she cared enough to be bothered, maybe she cared enough about me.

It was stupid. I realize that. But ever since then, it's sort of like the thrill of dating has lost its appeal. Which sucks, considering Jesse moved out of our house and into a house with Camilla. It's a little lonely at my place.

Which is good because I can put in the hours at work that I need to without being tied down to a woman.

"I don't think you believe me," I say.

"What? That you no longer have women coming out of your ears?" The tilt of Aria's brow as she concentrates on her computer screen tells me she's almost ready to drop this conversation.

"Yeah."

She shakes her head. "It's none of my business."

I shift in my stance. Talking about this isn't fun, but it needs to happen at some point, and because I'll be spending more time with Aria, I'm running with it now. "But you made it your business with Elisha."

"Who?"

My mouth clamps down hard before I open it again. "You remember the redhead? The one who has perfect aim with water bottle guns?"

Aria brings her fist up to her forehead, grinning. "That was so funny. You had it coming to you."

"I did. I deserved it and the breakup that happened that night as well."

"Oh. Sorry." A look of remorse coasts over her eyes before a smile dances at the corners of her mouth.

"You're not sorry," I counter.

She breathes half a laugh. "I'm not. Well, only because she deserved to know the truth."

"She did. She didn't deserve to be treated like that by me. I was a jerk. To her," I pause, "and to you."

She's not picking up what I'm laying down, that I really do feel bad about the way I was back then. "And to the leggy blonde at the wedding?" she asks.

"Yes, her, too. And I want you to know that the woman at the wedding, Gelsey? We've only ever been friends and she engages in PDA with everyone. Her aunt, slobbery kisses from her mini schnauzer, everyone."

"Okay. Makes sense," she says.

I can't read her right now, but I don't know if she believes me. And I hate that she can't trust me yet.

"Also, I wasn't trying to make you uncomfortable by bringing Elisha into the shop so soon after the first woman I brought in. I honestly thought it was Grammy's turn to work for Camilla that day, not you."

"So, you were hoping I didn't know you were dating her, so you could hit on me later?"

"No. That wasn't it."

Aria doesn't say anything, just quirks a small smile and hands me the plate. I thank her and go sit down.

I take a couple of bites and sigh again, this one barely suppressed. She's sitting on a barstool at the counter, concentrating on her laptop screen.

I can't hold it in any longer. "This cheesecake is incredible."

She nods and gives a polite smile, then returns to her computer.

I take another bite, unable to suppress another groan. "Seriously. It's the best I've ever had."

Her gaze sweeps over me with such intensity, I'm reminded of the photo shoot. My stomach does a flip-flop, exactly like it did when I saw the photo of us on the billboard. Exactly like it did when she was in my arms in that corseted dress.

"You know how we have to do that dinner for the committee and VIPs the week before the festival starts?" I say around a bite. I point at the cheesecake with my fork. "We should serve this. Camilla's a baking god."

Now a wide smile from Aria. "We need to figure out the main dish first, though. Maybe cheesecake won't even go with what we decide. Oh, and I got the budget information from them, the amount we can spend. Did you get that?"

"Yes. And I say we decide on something that goes with cheesecake, not the other way around."

She lifts a shoulder. "Maybe. We also need to figure out the details of the charitable donations to Santa's Helpers."

"Details like how we're going to present the funds to them, right?" I ask, remembering something about that in all the paperwork we were given. I focus on my last bite of cheesecake. I'll gladly pay for another slice.

"Yeah. I don't know if it's best to hand it over to them or to try to purchase a few toys or needed items with the money ourselves." She gets down from her barstool at the counter and walks around to my table. She laughs as she points to my plate. "You didn't eat the cheesecake the right way. You're going to have bad luck."

"Oh, right. Camilla's superstitious thing about pies and cheese-cakes." I laugh, remembering the first time she said something about it. "Never a dull moment. Which is good, because Jesse can be dull."

"That's not what Camilla thinks." Aria's got her hands jammed in her back pockets, and her apron is stained with raspberry and cherry glaze. "Anyway, we have to figure out those details for the charity."

I'd love to ask her out to discuss it over dinner, but I have a feeling if I say that, it will come off as being pushy. Or flirty. Or both.

"Let's discuss then." I lean back in my chair and thread my fingers together behind my head.

She gingerly takes a seat across from me. "Towards the back of the event tent, near the registers, the committee always puts up a large, four-feet-tall plastic Christmas stocking. It's borderline hideous, but that's part of the charm. There's a slot at the top where people can insert cash and gift cards for charity. Anyway, I think a personal touch is always nice. Taking a portion of the funds and buying presents for the kids sounds fun."

"I'll gladly live out my childhood fantasies at the toy store," I say. "We should try to get wish lists from Santa's Helpers, so we can get things we know the kids will like."

She nods, one brow cocked high. "Good idea. I can let the committee know we'd like to go in that direction."

"That committee, man," I say with a low whistle. "It's like an alternate universe."

She offers a gentle puff of a laugh. "I didn't know what I was getting into."

I rest my elbows on the table. "If you'd known, would you have said no? Do you regret being tied to me? Having to work with me?"

Her large brown eyes take me in. "I don't regret saying I'd join the committee. It'll be a good experience. A good chance to give back and learn a lot."

She didn't answer the question about me—and I hadn't meant for it to sound so needy.

We're saved from the awkwardness by Camilla, who enters the room in a rush.

"Good news, my friend! My uncle says you're free to stay at the apartment upstairs."

I look at Aria, who gives a cautious smile to Camilla. "Thanks. I don't think it will be for long. I can send your uncle a deposit and first and last month's rent. Whatever he needs."

"Since you're my friend, he said you'll only have to pay a deposit. Refundable when you move out, of course. No first and last month's rent required."

Aria lets out a breath. "That's great."

"What's happening? You moving in?"

"Well. Sort of." She swallows hard. "My grandpa's coming to live with my parents, so he needs the room I've been staying in."

I grin. "You live with your parents?" I knew she had in the past; I didn't realize she still did.

She shrugs. "After I graduated and came back to help Camilla run Shorty's, there weren't many options of places to live. I would have lived with Camilla, but at the time, her sister lived with her, and then a different roommate so they could split the rent. Besides, Rob was my social life. I didn't need any more of the college lifestyle, you know? And it's been okay to live with my parents."

"Ah. Rob. The boyfriend. Silent and unseen."

"What?" Her mouth bunches up as she raises her chin. "What about him?"

I chuff out a laugh. "I've never had the pleasure of meeting him." A flare of jealousy threatens.

"Too bad," Camilla says.

I don't miss the look she shoots me. Camilla doesn't like him, a fact that I greatly enjoy.

"Tell me about Rob. I've been dying to discuss him." I lean even more of my weight on the table. Call me weird, but I actually have been dying to run it by her. I have a sick fascination with seeing exactly what kind of read I can get on her relationship with this guy.

Her lower jaw moves back and forth before she meets my gaze. "You've been dying to discuss him? What's there to discuss?"

"Are you in love with him?"

Camilla raises her palms in the air and heads back to the kitchen. "Whoa. I'll get back to work while you two have this strange convo."

"I don't think that's any of your business," Aria says to me when Camilla's gone. Her eyes are thin slits.

Huh. She didn't say she was.

"Okay, okay. Fair. When's he coming back? Is he going to live in Arkansas forever?"

She kneads her forehead. "I don't know."

"Hey, let me know when you're moving. Since Rob's not around, I'd be happy to be your pack mule and help you with your stuff."

When Camilla darts back out of the kitchen to grab something, I say, "You know what's also good news, Camilla? This cheesecake. Easily the best I've ever had."

"Oh really?" She coos, and her gaze darts to Aria and then back at me.

"Yeah. When did you start serving it? Why is it just now getting in my belly? Because I could use a slice a day."

Aria smirks and her gaze runs up and down me.

"You may have a hollow leg, Theo, but your heart and blood pressure would be another story if you ate this cheesecake every day," Camilla says. "I'm glad you like it, though."

"It's …" I give a chef's kiss with my fingertips. "I'm getting emotional just thinking about it."

"Well, thank Aria. She made it." Camilla leaves for the kitchen again, and I can hear her chuckle from here.

Aria's biting back a smile.

Why does knowing this cheesecake came from her make her even more attractive than ever before?

Chapter 10

♥

Aria

The next morning, I'm up early, throwing stuff in boxes I brought home from Shorty's. Grandpa will be here in two short days, and now that I have a place to go, I've got to up my moving game.

When my parents told me my grandpa was coming here for an extended amount of time, they suggested I move into my sister's room and share with her. My sister is fine, as far as sisters go, but I don't want to share a room with a younger sibling now that I'm twenty-five years old.

Besides, I don't love that I'm still living with my parents. I'm supposed to be settling down and establishing myself. I'm supposed to be trying to break into my real career, the one I'll have forever, hopefully.

And when I say forever, there's still a small part of me that hopes I can intertwine that with a family of my own. Somehow.

First up? I need to move on from this bakeshop in a sketchy part of town.

That part of town is improving, though. An adorable toy store opened up down the block in time for the Christmas season. And in the late summer, a coffee shop and a sandwich place that hosts open mic nights came in up the street.

With Camilla getting the hang of running her own business and the quiet strength of Jesse in her life, I should feel ready to move on, to work in branding for a real firm, to be pushed and stretched more than I can be at Shorty's.

Soon. I can't quit now, with it being the busiest time of year. But I will. As soon as I can get up the courage.

Living above her shop should give me the courage I need, right? Then it won't be like I'm making a complete break.

I've packed four full boxes of my stuff by the time I hop in the shower and get ready for work. I can do this. It's time to move out—again—and get my footing in creating the life I want.

As I drive past the main entrance to the bakeshop, I see Liz Langer approaching our Christmas wreath-decorated doors. I hope she's not coming to the bakeshop to buy baked goods since we're still closed for another hour. Or is she here to visit me?

I find myself tidying my car for an inordinate amount of time after I park around the back next to Theo's car, wishing that, somehow, he would need to come back outside, and he and I could go face Liz together. She's a force to be reckoned with, and somehow, it's easier to manage her when Theo's there.

Which shouldn't be the case. I'm a grown woman. I don't need him or any other man to face Liz.

It's just that he has a way of putting people at ease—sometimes myself included. I can acknowledge that as fact.

And before I know it, I'll be moved in upstairs and Theo will be working right next door.

I'm not sure how I feel about that, and rather than sit and analyze, I decide to head in to see what Liz wants since Theo hasn't magically appeared.

I enter the shop, sling my apron on over my head, and can already hear her chatting with Camilla while I tie it on.

"Good morning!" Liz and Camilla both say to me, and then they drop their heads back in laughter.

"I heard her knocking and wondered if you'd parked in the front for some reason," Camilla says to me. "But no, it was Liz and she's come to track you down."

"Great." I offer a smile.

"Have you heard? About you and Theo?" Liz asks, beaming.

Anything involving Theo and I sends a thrill up my spine. And not necessarily the good kind of thrill. "No. But I'm hoping from your expression that it's good?"

Liz bumps out a laugh, types on her phone, and then hands it to me. "Look. We ran a few Facebook ads for the festival, standard procedure you know, and look at the comments we've been getting."

These two are HOT.

If guys actually looked this good in frock coats back in the 1800s, then where's a time machine? Because . . . dang!

Is anyone else hoping these two are a couple in real life? #relationshipgoals

"My personal favorite is . . ." Liz joins me behind the counter and scrolls down with her finger. "*If the Victorian guy and his lady are actually going to be at the festival, I'll come every day.*"

"Wow," I say. "This is shocking."

"Over two hundred comments! And counting." Liz beams again and then puts her arm around my shoulders. "Thank you for being willing to do this, Aria. I had a good feeling about you two, and already, you're exceeding my expectations."

"I hope it helps," I say. "Have any of the booths who withdrew decided to come back?"

Liz's face twists in frustration. "Not yet. But I'm hopeful they will. Or that we get even better ones signed up. We've reopened signups as of this morning, so that should get people talking. We've never done that before, and I think there are a lot of people who will jump on the opportunity."

"I bet that's true. Are you still getting fallout from the scandal?" I have to force a breath of air in my lungs. I read a few articles calling for a criminal investigation and some op-ed pieces wondering how the committee could have been so blind to these issues with Shoes and Dues for so long. If this trial by public opinion continues, there won't need to be a criminal investigation. People will boycott. And the festival might not survive.

"Some," Liz says. "But we're trying to stay positive. Keep our nose to the grindstone and not worry too much." She takes a deep, cleansing breath. "For tomorrow night's meeting, we'd love to hear your plans for the VIP dinner and more about Santa's Helpers."

"Of course." A flash of panic hits me. I can't get this wrong. I must be worthy of the blazer!

Thoughts of Theo in his blazer come up, unbidden.

Yum.

"Good," Liz says. "We'll see you then. And don't forget Friday's event."

Those comments about Theo and me have scrambled my brain, so it takes me a moment. "Oh! The night for the press, at Barrie Mansion?"

"Exactly. We'll need you there at six to get ready for the seven o'clock start time. Lots of details to go over so you can answer the press's questions. We'll have a few of our long-standing vendors there. And the high school concert choir will be there to sing a couple of catchy Christmas tunes. We're having one of the bus drivers bring over the risers Friday after school." Liz exhales and her mouth turns down in a frown. "Lots to do!"

I nod. "We'll be there."

"And thanks for your help with the rebranding. I know our marketing head appreciates the projects you've accepted so far."

I nod, but swallow hard.

Moving. Working for Camilla. Making appearances and doing design projects for the festival. Co-hosting and all that it entails. Avoiding Theo, which the above stuff isn't allowing me to do.

It's a lot. But it's all for a worthy cause, not the least of which is to add viability to my future branding career. "I'll keep doing what I can," I tell her.

And I will. I've always wanted this—to be involved in the inner workings of one of the happiest parts of my childhood. Besides, it's planting good seeds, positive vibes.

I just hope I don't lose my head in the process.

I also hope that Theo and I suddenly becoming this season's "It Couple" doesn't complicate things even more.

Chapter 11

Theo

I make my last moving trip of the day, in our first real snowstorm of the season, over to the new office building. It's not ideal to move my office stuff in my BMW because there is not a lot of room. And to be honest, I don't like driving it in the heavy snow. But I've carried all the boxes to my new office. And my pant cuffs that are wet from slipping in the snow will eventually dry, right?

My BMW is vintage, and I put a rebuilt engine in it. Buying a brand new, or even a used but fully functioning Beemer so early in my career? Ludicrous. But cars are my thing, specifically taking cars that used to be beautiful and making them beautiful again. Everything deserves a second chance. Heck, every*one* deserves a second chance, right?

Except Marty Fleming.

Marty Fleming is a dirt bag.

I'm not in the legal profession to help scum bags get off scot-free. I'm in the legal profession because I like to argue, in a controlled way, and because my mom was forced to quit her legal career far too early. I'm hoping my work can honor what she started out doing long ago. And the variety of cases at a small-town firm makes me feel like I am doing the worthwhile things my mom would have done if she'd been able to continue in the field.

Also? I'll be super transparent. Another reason I practice law: I don't like being poor.

Doing pro bono work, one of a handful of charity cases that Weatherby takes on every year because he's a decent human being, is okay. I like the money that the bigger family law stuff brings in, of course. But helping people in need has its own rewards.

When it's pro bono work for the likes of Fleming, however, it grates at my every last nerve.

This is our second meeting. The first one was in the county jail, and even though we've only just gotten started, his trial is in less than a month and we've got a lot to do.

"So, why don't you tell me the story one more time? And don't leave anything out."

He stares at my desk. He's got hat hair, an indented rim around his sandy-colored hair from the baseball cap he's just removed. "I didn't leave anything out before."

"I have to make sure, you know."

Marty nods. "I took the money from my boss's personal safe. I'd found a slip of paper on the floor with his combination written on it about a week before. I didn't know what it was at first, and I'm not sure why I kept it. But it dawned on me it could be the combo to his safe. Tried it out, and it opened. So I took the money. Not all of it. Just what I could grab." He clenches his jaw and runs a hand through his hair. "Had it in my car for two days. Couldn't stand it anymore, so I put it back. But my boss's assistant walked in. He thought I was taking it, not putting it back."

My insides begin to boil. I can't get invested in this, but the minute I stop caring about the person I'm working with is when I should give up the job and go do something else. At least that's what my favorite professor in law school always said.

And I'm trying to care. I am. It's just that he's giving off vibes that don't sit right with me.

"And how long ago did you abandon your family?" I ask.

I've got my face trained on my tablet, ready to fill in whatever answer he's going to give me. But I can see from the corner of my eye that his head has shot up in surprise at the question.

"I—" he stammers. "I guess I left the house two and a half months before I took the money. But what does that have to do with—"

"It has everything to do with it." I set down the tablet and stare at him. "The judge is going to see you as more than a guy who steals money from his employer, okay? It's going to look like more than a crime of opportunity. He's going to see you as the dregs of society.

You walk out on your wife and kids, don't give them any money. Your wife has to get another job, your oldest son has to forgo his plans for college so he can work and help support the family. All for what? So you can steal and then go to jail, leaving them even more desperate?"

He sighs and nods his head. "Yeah. Okay. I can see what you mean. My wife and I…we haven't been in a good place for a year or more. I didn't want to leave. It just got to the point where I felt like I had no other choice. So I got an apartment."

"There's always a choice. You can clean up. Get help for the drinking. Enroll in some financial planning classes. There are always things you can do. You don't have to skip town and go on your merry way, leaving your wife to put back the pieces. I heard you haven't given her a single dime since you left or since the arrest."

"What's your problem, man?" He stares at me a moment, his mouth in a hard line, before he shoots out a breath and rubs his nose with his thumb.

My chest burns. I realize why I hate the man so much. It's stupid I didn't see it before.

He did what my own father did.

Kind of.

And now I'm treating my client the way my father treated people.

Maybe Marty senses my realizations about myself because he calms down a little, too.

"You're right," he looks me in the eye, his voice more controlled. "Look. I'm not asking for any favors. I did take the money. I wanted to give it to my wife because she needed it for the kids' food and clothes. I did feel horrible I hadn't given her any money since I moved out. So I took it, and there are penalties I'm willing to pay." He rubs the back of his neck, and there are dark circles under his bloodshot eyes.

"But I wasn't keeping it," he says, "and I didn't spend any of it. I was putting it back when I got caught. I swear. So I'm hoping you can help the judge know the truth, so that I'm not serving more time than is necessary. I want to go home to my wife and try to pick up the pieces and make amends." His bottom jaw grates back and forth and he rubs above his eye. "I've been attending twelve-step meetings since I got out of jail. Hopefully that will help me get to a better place so I can fix my mistakes."

I sigh and rub the spot on my temple that's throbbing. I have a metal claw that's reaching from the base of my neck, all along my head, and clamping down on my forehead. "I'll do what I can." I push a form in front of him. "Take this home and fill it out in its entirety. Provide as much detail as you can. This will give me a better picture of what happened. And be sure to sign it and bring it back in the next day or two. We'll be in touch."

"Okay. Thank you." Marty meets my gaze. His is a tortured one.

I don't like this. I don't like the nuances that come with cases like this or defending someone who's guilty.

Still, I offer him a smile, as best as I can. I want to work hard for him. I want to do my part. I just can't stop seeing my dad's face when I look at him.

And next time I get assigned a pro bono case, I hope it's something like social security or tax issues. Almost anything would be better than this.

"You got everything you need in here?" Jay Knowles, Weatherby's son-in-law and partner, pops his head into my new upstairs office later that day.

"It's a dream come true!" I hold out my arms enthusiastically. "Look at it. A lot of potential."

I mean what I'm saying. Yeah, the space is less than half the size of the downstairs offices. And I don't exactly love being the only person upstairs. I like the hive mind and having lots of people in and out.

But it's a fresh slate, with new carpet, paint, a balcony, and a lot of possibilities.

And . . . Aria's apartment is right next door. That's a bonus, too.

"It's nice." Knowles says, collapsing in a chair I've stationed across the desk from mine. "My wife is coming in this weekend to spruce my space up. She didn't want me to bring over anything from the old building except for the photos of the fam, you know? She's got all these visions in her head."

I can read between the lines. "Expensive visions?"

He laughs in agreement. "Uh huh. But she insists it will help with client retention. So I'm trying to go with it."

"How are your cases?" I ask him. "Anything you need to workshop?"

Right now, I'd much rather think about his instead of my own, especially Fleming's theft case.

He nods. "Mediation in the morning. Hopefully it goes smoothly. Pops says I'm ready. How's the theft case?"

"Pops" is Weatherby to Knowles, and I feel a stir of discomfort when I hear him say it. I'd like to call my boss "Pops." I've almost said it a time or two, but I always chicken out.

"It's going, I guess." I change the subject. "Still waiting for the green light on the Dahlen case." There's a sour taste in my mouth. "Wish I could start preparing, but I don't have access to anything yet. You heard anything?" I swear, if Weatherby gives the mother lode Dahlen prenup and will case to Knowles . . .

"Aleecia Dahlen came in this morning, but Pops is still trying to hold her off. I don't know what he's waiting for."

"He might be stalling because he's waiting for me to get more done with the festival," I tap out my anxieties with my fingers on the desk.

Knowles laughs. "He knows you're working on it. You always do." He chews on the corner of his bottom lip and makes a show of pulling at his collar, like he's nervous about trying to keep up. "Besides, your face is all over every billboard in town."

My neck heats up. "Yeah. I think that's proof enough right there."

"How did you get so unlucky? I had to volunteer last year and all I was assigned to do was take tickets at some fancy dinner and cashier for a couple of days at the festival."

"You lucky son of a gun." I blow a raspberry and scrunch up my face. "Well, you didn't have the good fortune of volunteering at the exact moment that somebody decided to cause a scandal and get ousted."

"I heard about Carl and Amanda," Jay says. "That's pretty heartless, taking the money meant for the kids for all their quote, unquote overhead."

I shake my head. "It is. I guess Aria and I happened to be at the wrong place at the wrong time."

Knowles laughs. "I do not envy you. But it's only for a few more weeks. Come Christmas Eve, the festival's all over."

Why does that thought make me miss Aria already? What is that all about? She doesn't like me and has a boyfriend. There's no need to wish for things that aren't going to happen.

Outside and down below, I hear a screech of metal on metal. Knowles cringes. "What's going on out there?"

I yank the strings on the blinds covering the window, and smile at the scene below.

It's Aria. And it looks like she needs a rescuer.

I'm more than happy to oblige.

Chapter 12

Aria

My two-drawer, metal filing cabinet, the one that holds my graphic design dream board items, decides to pitch a fit right as I'm easing it onto the dolly I've borrowed from my neighbor. It topples forward, screeches its front down the tailgate of my dad's truck, and lands upside down with a lightning crack onto the pavement.

I don't exactly know what to do about this, except for stare up at the white, snowy sky, take a deep breath, and hope I can hoist it up enough to get it properly situated on the dolly.

Yes, I had several offers for help with my move. Camilla and Jesse both offered, as well as my brothers, and my dad. But none of them could help until at least six p.m., and I wanted to get a move on.

I laugh at the little pun I'd made in my mind. Get a move on while I'm moving? Clever!

Any way you slice it, I should have waited, as is evidenced by my sorry stack of images and cut outs from the cabinet scattered all over the ground. But when it's time to get the thing done, I just want to get the thing done.

Grandpa's flying in from Boca Raton late tonight, and I wanted to have everything out of the room and cleaned up for him. I can't wait to give him a hug.

But moving's already exhausting. I frown at my filing cabinet. I totally should have waited for some help.

I manage to gather up the items that landed in the snow and close the drawer back up. Then, I brush off the snow that's dusted the top of a box in the back of the truck. I heft the box into my arms, rotate to face the employee entrance of Shorty's and run smack into a tall, dark, handsome . . . Theo?

"Whoa." He grasps the box to steady it. "Hey moving buddy! I moved in today, too." His grin is wide.

"Moving buddy?" I blow a puff of air up to try to move the lock of hair that's escaped from my headwrap and fallen over my face. It doesn't work.

"Here, allow me."

He's adopted his horribly bad British accent again and even dropped the *H* sound altogether. This time, a laugh rushes out of me.

"I've got it. But I'd love some help with the filing cabinet." I motion towards it with my head as I try to step past him.

He blocks my progress. "Gladly," he says, then reaches a hand up to my face. "Except first, this . . ." He takes the lock of hair in my eyes and gently brings it around so that it's pinned out of my way. "There. Now there's not so much of a hazard going on."

I feel exposed, vulnerable, my skin still warm where his fingers brushed against it. "Thanks," I say, my gaze catching his. In the brisk November air, his eyes are bright blue.

I've never noticed how vivid they are. It must have something to do with the light today.

He jogs to open the back door of Shorty's for me. Once he's sure I can safely tackle the steep, narrow flight of stairs directly off the door, I hear his footfalls crunch in the snow behind me as he jogs back to my dad's truck.

I manage the steps okay and sigh with relief as I see that Camilla's propped the apartment door open for me at the landing. Easing my way through the door with the big box blocking most of my vision, I enter the small kitchen. I set the box down on the table, which is a solid, deep cherry wood.

I take a moment to still my breathing and the thought occurs to me that seeing Theo so suddenly might have caused more of a breathing issue than carrying the box up the stairs.

But that won't do at all. I can't fall for Theo, not in the least because he's already fallen for all sorts of women all over town.

Except, according to him, he's out of that phase. I don't know what to make of that possibility, so I focus on my new digs instead.

Camilla and I were up here last night cleaning, but now, I see it with fresh eyes. Even though it's small, it's mine. I've only ever lived with college roommates or my family, so it's a whole new world, which makes me think of that song about unbelievable sights and indescribable feelings. I want to glide through the rooms and hallways singing the blockbuster Disney song while I admire my very own toilet, my very own doorstops, and my very own kitchen sink complete with a dish drainer and half a bottle of Dawn.

The small front room has a matching bright-blue velour sofa and loveseat set and a bookcase painted in a complementary yellow. In the kitchen, there are dark-cherry cabinets and a silvery tin Mexican-style backsplash. The floors are grey tile, and down the hall is a bathroom and bedroom. I like the old-fashioned plaid wallpaper, dark wainscoting, and the narrow door leading to the black iron-railed balcony. It's small, and the view is unremarkable—it's only the alley parking lot.

But it's mine.

I step onto the balcony and look down through the falling snow at my dad's truck. Theo's nowhere to be seen, the dolly abandoned near the back door down below. When I hear heavy footfall up the steps, I rush to try to help him. He's holding the office green filing cabinet on its side in both arms like a sack of potatoes and it's blocking most of his ability to see.

"Whoa. You couldn't wait for some help?" I toss out, guiding him with my voice and non-helpful arm and hand gestures. I try to ignore the very real bulging of muscles in his arms and the way his shoulders widen with the weight of the cabinet.

"Try" being the operative word. I have to tear my eyes away.

"Where do you want it?" he grunts out.

"Uh, just anywhere is fine."

He rotates to one side to give me a pointed look. "Can you tell me where you'll be keeping it?" he asks between gritted teeth. "Then we won't have to move it again later."

"Well, how about in the bedroom?"

With a nod, he carries it down the hallway.

"It's the last door on the right," I tell him before he goes inside.

"In the corner?" he asks, his voice strained.

"Yes. Sure." I cringe. I bet he's going to have a bulging disc in his spine after this.

He bends his knees and shoves it out and down, and it lands on the carpet with a thud. The front's all scratched from the tailgate . . . and my stupidity.

Theo is breathing heavily, and he wipes his forearm across his brow. "What's in there?"

"Only about twenty plus years of design ideas I tore from magazines or printed off." I trap my lower lip between my teeth.

"Design? Like graphic design?"

"All kinds, really. And some branding ideas, some favorite works of art. I've got it divided into files and sorted by years and styles. It's been my hobby for so long, I couldn't part with it." I chew on the inside of my cheek.

"Show me," he says, and he's almost caught his breath. It's like he's a sprinter and he's just finished a race. His business casual clothing, with the fitted tan button-down shirt and mocha-colored pants—which are also fitted, a fact that I'm trying not to care about—suit him nicely. They complement his relaxed personality and decidedly unrelaxed body quite well, even if they're damp from the snowy cabinet.

I wave him away. "There's nothing that would interest you, Theo. It's just my whims. Things that caught my eye, that resonated with me over the years."

"I want to know what resonates with you." He's saying it with such a serious expression, without even a hint of sarcasm or flirtation. Does he really want to know?

Against my better judgement, I go to the top drawer, push the silver button near the handle, and pull, wiggling it because it got jammed from the damage. "Let's see. You want to know what I liked senior year of college?"

I move my hair out of my way with the back of my hand and reach for the appropriate file. It's jam packed with all kinds of random things: ads from the school newspaper that I liked, some class assignments, random stickers, matchbooks, even a napkin from a restaurant with a cool design.

"What's this?" Theo's behind me, and he's tall enough that he can reach over my shoulder. He grabs something from the file.

My heart leaps into my throat when I see what he's holding. A cut out of an assignment from a class. It's Rob and me, toothy grins, and I photoshopped it, adding a rain drop treatment over the top.

I take a deep breath. "That's Rob. I did it for an assignment."

It takes me a minute to turn and meet Theo's gaze, but when I do, his brows are raised, his eyes questioning. "I don't mean for this to sound weird or anything, but he's a handsome man."

I shunt out a laugh. "Thanks. I guess?"

I grab it from his hand, and he groans. "Now, let me finish." He cranes his neck to look at the photo again. "He's not bad looking. But you. You're . . . radiant."

He's called me enchanting before. And now I'm radiant?

I shake my head and try to put the photo back in the file, but he stops me.

"No," he says, gently drawing up the photo again. The edges of our hands are touching as we both hold it. His gaze goes from it to me, drinking me in. It's one of curiosity, of yearning. "Do you not see it?" he asks quietly. "Do you not know how beautiful you are?"

I could chalk it up to Theo being Theo, but the slash of cold, hard truth that he sees me, that he's closely aware of me? That's what skewers me. He's genuinely curious, if I understand what he sees—what he thinks.

I don't know how to answer his question—it feels impossible to know how.

"I also think this Rob guy doesn't appreciate you," he says. A nerve under his eye twitches.

I find my voice. "Why do you say that?" I should tell him it doesn't matter since Rob and I broke up.

"Because if I were him?" His laugh is a grunt in his throat. "I'd never go to Arkansas and be gone for years. I'd have had a hard time leaving you for a single day."

I want to say something in response to his gaze that's equal parts territorial, kind, and with a hint of disgust at Rob. I shove the photo back in the folder and quickly slide it back into place in the drawer. "So anyway, now you know what's in there."

I want to tell him we broke up, but I've only told Camilla and Grandpa, asking them to keep it to themselves. The truth of everything clogs my throat, and I swallow hard.

As if Theo's words haven't done enough, seeing that photo of Rob and me disarms me. When I look at that photo? It's like I'm looking at two complete strangers.

My stomach turns. I don't even remember how I felt when that photo was taken. I don't remember having strong feelings for him.

It's all too uncomfortable, especially with Theo here, and his words curving throughout all the pockets of my mind. There are pockets of the past, of my decisions—right and wrong. Pockets of what I want. Pockets of what I can't have.

And somehow, Theo's mixed up in all of them.

I clear my throat. "I better go get the rest of my boxes. My grandfather's flying in late tonight and I need to get his room ready."

"Wait. Wait just a second." Theo's got a light in his eyes that speaks of mischief.

He walks over to the wall across the room and knocks on it a couple of times. Then, he turns to the narrow door and opens it. He steps onto my balcony.

"Nice view of the backsides of old buildings, eh?" I joke as I join him, the bitter cold of Colorado air biting into me already. My heart has only started to slow back to a normal rate since he told me I'm beautiful and that he couldn't stand leaving me for a single day.

That is, if he'd been in Rob's position.

Now those pockets in my head are filling up, stuffed with so many amendments and agreements. So many attempts to fill in the blanks and answer all the questions.

"Wait right here," he says, backing away. He keeps his eyes trained on me, like I'm a wild animal and might bolt at any minute. When I can't help the smallest of smiles, he turns and hurries back through the door and out of my bedroom.

"Okay," I say under my foggy breath as I wrap my arms around me. Delicate and soft snowflakes begin to fall again in the ether around me.

Only a minute later, I hear the scrape of a door opening. He steps onto the balcony next to me—only six feet away.

"Hey, hey neighbor," he says with a laugh, the set of his brow bringing a triumphant look to his face.

"That's your office?" I point to his balcony door.

"That's right, dahling," he says in a crisp British accent.

Seriously? Now I'm sharing a wall—and a view—with Theo Carter?

Chapter 13

Theo

As she looks at me from her balcony, Aria's thick, chestnut hair hangs to one side, catching crystals of snow as she gives up a delicious laugh.

"So. We're sharing a wall, huh?" she says. "And we have identical balconies."

Yes. Yes, we are. And yes, we do.

"And I have a lot of work piling up, so I'll be here for some long hours," I say. I can't help the grin that's splitting my face. What could be better than daydreaming of Aria in the room next to me?

But I need to rein it in, recall my frivolous and indulgent thoughts back.

"Hey, maybe we could rig up a basket system and you could pass me some cheesecake when I get a hankering for it," I say, grasping for a casualness I don't feel. "You know, like a dumbwaiter that works horizontally?"

She clicks her tongue. "If you want cheesecake, you can come next door and pay for it like a civilized person."

"Gladly. But I could pass you some cash with the basket."

She shakes her head, but her smile is wide. "You're impossible. I better go finish moving in. Thanks for bringing my filing cabinet up for me." She presses her palm to her forehead. "Is your back okay?"

"It's fit as a fiddle," I say, and then cringe. This time my accent sounds more Irish than British.

I should just stop now. I'll chalk it up to nerves.

I told her she was beautiful, and that Rob chump was an idiot. Not in so many words. But there was something there between us, a more powerful pull than I've felt with anyone. All the people I've dated casually have been blips on the radar of my life. They've fulfilled the measure of exactly what I'd hoped for—nothing more than a momentary distraction.

But Aria? Ever since I laid eyes on her two years ago, she's been an ever-present thrum on my consciousness. She's on a whole other plane than anyone I've known. And after my last breakup months ago, I've been trying to figure out how to move past this fascination with her. She's with someone else and the jealousy and anger that comes with that knowledge just might do me in.

I meant what I said. She's beautiful, yes. But she's also underappreciated by the man who should be giving her his whole world. To me, that's unacceptable.

I can't bring all this up now, though, especially as we're standing a few feet apart on our respective balconies, freezing our booties off.

"Well. Bye." She offers a little beauty-queen wave and ducks her head back inside.

She better not think I'm done helping her.

I hear someone clear their throat behind me, so I stand up straight and turn to see Weatherby in the doorframe.

"Is there a problem with the balcony?" Weatherby asks.

"Oh, no. Not at all." I give the railing a solid pat before moving to walk back into my office. "Do you need any help getting your furniture in?"

Weatherby shakes his head as he steps aside to let me through. "I've hired it out, and they're almost done." His gaze goes around the room. "I almost envy you, being the only one to have an office on the top floor. It's nice and quiet up here. And you get a little balcony."

"But your office is three times the size."

"Yeah." He sits down on the chair across from my desk. "It's a nice building. I hope it ends up being a smart move for business."

I swallow hard. This was my idea, one that, to be honest, I'm sometimes surprised came to fruition. When Jesse told me several months ago about the movement to revitalize this section of downtown and all the kickbacks businesses could get if they relocate, I told Weatherby all about it. I knew he'd been looking to either move or remodel, and the idea of being next to Camilla's bakeshop, and therefore, my brother, was appealing.

And yeah. I wanted to be near Aria's work. Now she's living here, too. Bonus!

"I think it's going to be great for business," I say. "The office is super nice."

And I wouldn't trade offices with Weatherby now. Because this is a good situation. I like being right next to Aria's new place. I like having twinning balconies.

Weatherby nods, and I can tell he's deep in thought about something else.

"Is there anything else you'd like to discuss?" I ask.

"Well." He sighs. "The Fleming case concerns me."

The race of blood pumping in my ears matches the unease that rushes to my stomach, which isn't anything new when it comes to thinking about Marty Fleming and his case. "How so?"

"I've looked over your hours. I'm surprised at the low number. And the court date is approaching."

I could offer any excuse I can think of, and there are a few that pop up instantly. But I'm not interested in making my career by using excuses.

"You're right. I apologize. I'll make it right. I'll ramp it up."

"I'd appreciate that." He frowns. "These pro bono cases are important, Theo. Fleming deserves every bit as much as we give our paying clientele." His eyes soften and his shoulders round. "Look, I started my career doing this kind of defense work in Sacramento. Sometimes people just need someone to believe in them, you know?"

This is a side of Weatherby I've only seen when his grandkids come and visit the office, and he turns into a big marshmallowy teddy bear, carrying them around and giving them piggyback rides and letting them raid his candy drawer.

It's great. But all the other times, he's a hard hitter, which I've always thought is what makes him a good attorney. Now I'm not exactly sure I know what motivates him.

"I guess it's difficult for me," I say. "He's guilty. He did take that money."

The smile he gives me holds pity, like I'm a little slow to understand. "And he was putting it back. Which doesn't make it okay. I know he needs to do some time. But this is a complex case."

"Do you really believe him?" I scoff. "That he was putting it back when he got caught? I'm not so sure."

"Doesn't matter. Our job as his representation isn't to decide that. It's to present his case as he's presented it to us, using our knowledge of the law to the best of our ability. That's what—well, I was going to say that's what he's paying us for, but I guess he's not paying us, is he?" He shakes with full-belly laughter.

Talking of payment makes me think of the Dahlen prenup and will amendments, and my blood gets pumping even more, salivating over this high-profile, high-income opportunity.

Not that I'm going to mention it. I've made it clear I want it, and Mrs. Dahlen has made it clear she wants me to represent her. I have to be patient with Weatherby until he's ready to officially hand it over to me.

He unbuttons his sleeves and rolls them up to his elbows. He's sensitive to heat, and I'm guessing my upstairs office is too warm for him. "How's the festival?" he asks. "I trust you're representing the firm well?"

There he is. The hard hitter has returned.

"Yes, I am. Have you seen the billboards and posters around town? My brother says they're up even in Denver." I smile as I think of Aria in that red velvet dress.

"I have. Not what I was thinking would happen when I handed it over to you, but this can be a good thing for all involved."

I almost add that it's one of the reasons I haven't been doing enough on the Fleming case, but I check myself. Again, no excuses.

And plus, is that why? Or am I dragging my feet for other reasons? Reasons I can't fully understand, but I know have to do with my family's past.

Ding, ding, ding. That's it, of course.

But I've got to step up and do this, if not for Fleming, for Weatherby, the firm, and my career as a whole.

That doesn't mean I can't run back over to Shorty's and finish helping Aria first.

Chapter 14

Aria

With Theo's help, I get everything from the truck into my new apartment in less than an hour, and I'm heading back to my parents' house to get the rest. A smile tweaks the corners of my mouth as I remember how he looked on his balcony near mine.

Handsome. Charming. Happy.

No wonder the man has women eating out of the palm of his hand. I see the appeal of Theodore Vincent Carter.

Okay, okay, Universe. I get it.

But it comes down to this: he's not the staying kind, and I don't need all the fuss and craziness. Theo's dramatic. I'm allergic to relational drama.

He's intense. He's engaging. He's the kind of man who's all in, in everything he does.

And I can't.

I can't, Theo.

I want to. I'll admit that. But like my mom says, people change. And Theo's the type of man who, if I let myself climb all in and he changes? Changes his mind, changes who he is?

I'll never be okay again.

I shake my head and pull into my parents' driveway. My dad and brothers aren't home from work yet, but that's alright. I can do this myself—except for the bed. And yes, Theo offered to come with me, but I told him not to worry about it. I know he said he had a lot of work to do.

With several trips back and forth from my soon-to-be former bedroom and the truck, I've got everything packed up by six. My family comes home and helps me with the bed. And even though they drive over to the apartment with me to get it up the stairs, Theo's out of his office within seconds of us arriving, ready to help again, all bright-eyed and bushy-tailed. It doesn't take long for him to win over my dad and brothers with his charisma and enthusiasm.

The man is determined and sunny, I'll give him that.

Since when did I become the pessimist around here? Nerves and a sense of hollow dread soak me.

This life, my life . . . I'm just not quite the person I'd imagined I'd be at this point.

I want so much more than what I'm allowing myself to have. I want to be so much more.

Camilla comes up to my new apartment as soon as she closes the shop, and Theo brings us all sandwiches and drinks to keep us fueled. Bless the man, the ham and Swiss, and the grape electrolyte drink he brought me. But now he's gone, needing to make some visits for a case he's working on.

So why can I not get him out of my head while Camilla and I are folding my clothes neatly and putting them in my dresser drawers?

Frustration bubbles up again. I've got to stop this.

It's nearly ten p.m. when I finish getting as much situated in my new place as is possible in one day.

After giving Camilla a bestie hug, I head back over to my parents' house and get my room cleaned up for my grandpa while they go pick him up at the airport.

I light a cinnamon Christmas candle in the room and decorate the windows with strings of holly leaves and berries. And when he gets in, at almost midnight, he hugs me with a Santa-like "Ho, ho, ho!" His wiry frame is draped in a thermal shirt, a flannel button-down, and a cardigan.

My sister works early in the mornings at her on-campus job, so she's asleep. But my parents, Grandpa, and I enter the living room with his luggage.

"You're ready for Colorado winters," I tell him, reaching over to straighten his navy cardigan.

"I traded in my beach Speedo for these sick threads." He strikes a few model poses, and when he turns around and places his hands on his hips, I see his grey hair is still mussed up from the airplane ride. My parents sigh as if to say, "*What have we gotten ourselves into?*"

"I wish you were kidding about the beach Speedo, but somehow, I know you're not." I'm grinning. That's another thing about being around Grandpa. By the time I go back to my apartment, I know I'll have sore abs from laughing.

"Just cause I didn't wear it when you visited me, doesn't mean it doesn't exist." He uses his pointer finger to slide his glasses back up his nose.

"Well, you look nice," I say, eyeing him carefully. He does, and besides being a little thinner, he doesn't seem to have aged at all since I last saw him during our visit a year ago.

We sit on the sofa and my parents follow in the chairs opposite us. "How's your mother?" Grandpa asks my mom. He's referring to my grandmother, his ex-wife.

Howard and Mischla Beckwith split up before I was even born, and she's been married twice since then, while grandpa has chosen the bachelor lifestyle, permanently at this point, it seems.

"She's well," my mother says, adjusting the clip in which she's pulled back half of her greying, thick hair. "She and Byron have divorced, but you probably know that, Dad."

He nods slowly. "She still in Milwaukee?"

"For the time being. I wonder if she'll move though, since she's not with Byron anymore. She needs to. She needs to be closer to family," Mom chides, clicking her tongue.

"Erin," my father says, disdain in his tone. "She's fine. She likes her life there."

"Does she, though? She's always unhappy." My mom frowns. "Maybe she's lonely and doesn't want to admit it."

"Let her figure things out on her own," Dad says. "She doesn't need us interfering."

Mom rears back, eyeing him through thin slits. "You just don't want her coming to live with us or near us, is that it?"

My dad gives a humorless laugh. "I've let your father come here. Why not your mother? What about your sister and brother? They can come too, and it will be a huge Beckwith party." His smile doesn't meet his eyes. He's in sarcastic mode, one of my least favorite versions. My stomach flips the same way it always did growing up.

"You'd dare say that with my dad just arriving? He's sitting right here." She throws her hands in the air. "I can't believe you can't be more cordial right now."

"I'm just saying, you can stop meddling. Your mom's fine. Everything's fine."

"Yeah? Everything. Like our marriage?" My mom crosses her arms over her middle. "We're unhappy, Dean."

"Wow. That escalated quickly," I say.

At this, several things happen at once. The cat goes darting from the room. My dad stands up, the chair sliding back from him in a loud scrape across the hardwood floor. My mom's jaw is hard set, her aura is seething. They're ready to start their verbal war.

Grandpa and I stand, too. Redness has started creeping up from under the collar of his shirt.

"Come on. I'll help you bring your stuff into the room." But my voice isn't working quite right on account of the ball that's formed in my throat.

Here's one excellent reason I've moved out of the house. My parents mostly live their own separate lives, only interacting when necessary. But every once in a while, it's World War Three around here.

We head down the hall to his new room, and Grandpa sits on the corner accent chair. "This room is great!" he says. "I appreciate you giving it up for me. And your parents for letting me stay, although I have a feeling I'm not gonna be here too long." He points in the direction of the living room. "Tough crowd." He smiles, but I see the pain in his eyes.

I tilt my head towards the hallway. "I'm really sorry about that. They're usually not—" I stop myself. Why try to sugar coat it? Why say something that isn't true? "Well, they usually keep it under wraps."

"I understand. And it's okay. They've had a hard road in their marriage. At least they're sticking it out. Something I couldn't manage to do with your grandmother." He licks his lips as if he's trying to get rid of a bitter taste.

Is their sticking it out a good thing, though?
Maybe.

There's a lot I don't know. But one thing is sure: In my family, love usually equals misery.

Chapter 15

Theo

"Do you have all my paperwork, Theo?" Aleecia Dahlen asks me, sitting across from my desk. She grabs a lock of her red hair and rotates it nervously around her finger.

I finally got the greenlight to work on the Dahlen case. When I got the good news yesterday, I felt like Maxwell Smart when he thought he was in the Cone of Silence. I could have screamed how happy I was and even added in a couple of hitch kicks for fun, too.

In her mid-fifties, and wearing a trim blue suit, Aleecia barely looks forty. "I'd like to get a jump on both the will and the prenup. The sooner this is done, the better." She bites her bottom lip. "Not that I should rush anything, and the wedding's not for a few more months. I just have to be sure to protect myself." She waves me off. "My therapists say my nerves are normal."

"Therapists? Plural?"

"No one should have to get by these days with only one. I have my personal one, our couple's counselor, my life coach, my group therapist, my yogi therapist . . ." She trails off.

Normally, I'd disagree with her on that one, figuring one solid counselor is all a person needs. But right now? I feel so mixed up with my obsession to make partner someday and all these unnecessary, and frankly, borderline frustrating thoughts of Aria, that maybe Aleecia Dahlen is on to something.

I nod. "I feel for you. This isn't easy. But you've done the right thing coming to us."

"I learned my lesson." She gives a half-hearted laugh. "For my other marriage, I didn't sign a prenup and the divorce took over two years to settle. Please. I can't go through that again."

"I don't want that for you, either." I offer a smile. "This is a happy occasion, Aleecia. You're getting married."

A smile spreads across her lacquered lips. "I am. And I even toyed with the idea of not doing a prenup, if you can believe it. Ronald and I fell in love before he even understood my wealth and, I don't know, he's not intrinsically motivated by money. It almost felt safe to not even worry about this. But then I woke up."

"So, how did you and Ronald meet?" I'll admit it to no one, but I personally love hearing people's love stories. *Other* people's love stories.

Her gaze dips to the floor and she smiles. "I was spending the winter down in Arizona with my sister. I signed up to take a literature class at a community college down there, you know, something fun and different for me to do. I always loved my English classes in my undergrad. Well, Ronald was my professor. When the course was over, he asked me out and we fell in love. He's so professor-like. He wears these awful polos and only has a couple of pairs of shoes, if you can believe it. But he writes me poetry."

She glances up at me. "Poetry, Theo. He's the best thing to ever happen to me, and I love him so much. He's my other half. So, yes, I've been dragging my feet on this whole prenup thing. I really hope it isn't necessary, and I don't want to jinx anything."

"I hope you never have to even consider it again once it's drawn up. Your portfolio is complicated, though. And like you said, you don't want a repeat of before. Look, you can be generous in your prenuptial agreement. It doesn't have to be doom and gloom."

"I feel like I have enough to go around. Enough that we'd both be happy, you know? Except if we split up, I—" her voice catches. "I wouldn't be happy at all."

My stomach rolls. I do know. As a child of divorce, I get it. "When you think of it, this is an act of love. If the unthinkable happens, and I'm betting it won't, you don't want to be dragging each other through endless court dates and fights. It just makes sense."

I lean back in my chair, my gaze going swiftly around the room. I wish I'd had time to spruce it up a little before she came. Maybe decorate with some Christmas wreaths or something. If it were up to me, I'd never decorate for Christmas, but in New Hedge, that's akin to fraud. Or stealing someone's eggnog.

"How does Ronald feel about the idea?" I ask.

She shrugs. "He's fine with it. Says he doesn't care about my money. The funny thing is? I actually believe him." She looks guilty, like she's almost ashamed that she believes her fiancé loves her for her and not her wealth.

What kind of a sad world do we live in? I give an internal bitter laugh. I'm cynical when it comes to love, too.

"He sounds wonderful. I can't wait to meet him." I pat the files. "We can go over the basics today, and then I'll spend the next few days going over all of your documents. Then we can meet again next week, if that works for you? You're welcome to bring him then, or you can wait until another meeting."

"I know it's a lot." She fingers the edge of one of the sheets of paper. "And there's more that my accountants sent you digitally, as well. Let me know if you need anything else, especially to rework my will."

The set of her jaw tells me she's paid a dear price for the money she has.

"I may have inherited a large sum," she says. "But I've grown it for the last thirty years and I'm not naïve about money. I just hope I'm not naïve about love this time around." She perks up a smile and runs a hand through her red tresses. When she stands from the desk, she tilts her head. "Working as a family attorney probably makes it difficult for you to believe in love, huh?"

I grunt out a laugh of surprise. "No, my father took care of that for me, all on his own. I actually really like family law, though."

She thanks me and leaves, and I get a thrill looking at the paperwork detailing all the ways in which her wealth has been diversified. This is going to be fun.

And I really do wish her the best. I just can't get behind the whole love-thing for myself, although if Aria would ever dump that Rob guy, and if the world was a different place entirely, she might be the one to snap me out of that.

My eyes are going cross eyed, but it's okay. I enjoy the Dahlen paperwork. Yes, some aspects of the law can be incredibly snore-inducing. But there are times when writing contracts gets complex and I love a good puzzle.

It's dark outside when I hear Aria come home. A door creaks on its hinges, and I realize it's probably her bedroom door. I had enough of a hard time helping her set up her bed the other day. It was difficult to not think about her sleeping in it, how she might look. And now, every time I hear her in her room, it's going to be difficult to control my thoughts. She's a beautiful woman—strong, smart, and interesting.

I hear doors and drawers opening and closing. These walls must be thin. I don't know how I feel about that. Can I be annoyed, excited, and frustrated all at the same time?

Water's running through the pipes, and I'm tripped up by the sound of the minutiae of Aria getting ready for bed. It's nine o'clock. Does Aria go to bed early?

I'm back into the Dahlen work when I hear her blow her nose. Why is nose blowing kind of cute all the sudden? Soon, she blows her nose again, and I wonder if she's coming down with a cold.

And that's when I hear a sob. Maybe what I'm hearing is her TV. Then, it comes again, and I know instinctively that it's her.

Aria's crying.

Oh man. This is territory that I'm not exactly comfortable with. My first instinct is to ignore it. Mature? No. But I'm not very well-equipped with this sort of thing. I don't have sisters, unless you count Camilla now. And I don't date women long enough to get to the crying stage of a relationship. I don't even have relationships to speak of, so this is out of my comfort zone.

I take a deep breath and assess. Okay. So she's crying. And I'm sad about that. I wonder what happened.

Maybe her boyfriend kicked the can? Maybe he had a freak accident?

And then I scold myself when I feel a thrill of excitement at that thought.

Geesh, Theo. That's terrible of you.

I turn my focus back to the contracts for Aleecia Dahlen, but I hear Aria again and she's definitely crying.

Crap.

Every cell inside of me that came with being born a male rallies the troops at the sound of her crying. This woman is sad. She might need help. I can save her. I can be her knight in shining armor.

I knock on the wall, softly at first so I don't startle her. I think she's stopped, maybe straining to hear if that was really a knock or not? I don't know, but I knock again, this time a little louder.

"Aria? Are you okay?" I say through the wall.

I hear an intake of breath. "Oh," she shouts loudly through the wall. "I'm sorry you can hear me." I've never heard a voice blushing before, but it's happening now. There's a rustle on the bed and the springs coil and squeak.

"No. I mean. You're obviously not okay." I rest my forehead against the wall. I'm truly bad at this kind of thing. "And it's not bothering me at all. That's not why I ..." I sigh, hot and short. "I thought I'd see if you needed anything?"

There's another rustle, and then her voice comes in louder and more clear—closer to mine. "No. I don't need anything." She sounds like she has a stuffy nose from the crying.

"I have a big box of tissues right here. I could rig up a basket and pulley and lever system and—"

"For the last time, the dumbwaiter idea is not going to work." She sounds exasperated, and I can't help but smile.

I laugh. "Okay, okay. Dream killer." I scratch at my jawline, wondering what to say next. "What's got you down?"

"I'm not going to shout my pitiful problems through a wall, Theo."

"How about from balcony to balcony?" I shout. I slide my coat on and grab the blanket I brought for this very purpose from my bottom desk drawer. I step outside.

Winters in Colorado, man. It's inhumane.

I wait for longer than is comfortable. Heck, nothing about this is comfortable.

Finally, her door opens, and she steps out. Her face is red, and her eyes are puffy. She's wearing a brown pullover with matching joggers.

I ball up the blanket and toss it to her. She catches it with a quizzical look.

"I brought it after the last time we rendezvoused on the balconies. Figured you'd stay out here longer with me if you were warm." I shrug.

"Thanks, Theo." She shakes out the blanket and wraps it around her shoulders. She sighs. "Why are you still at work?"

"I'm in the zone and getting paid a pretty penny, so why not?"

"I heard you work pretty hard over there."

There's no sarcasm in her voice.

"Aw, is my sister-in-law saying nice things about me?"

"Never." Her hard smirk makes me laugh.

And then, she smiles. It's barely there, but I'm counting it as real.

"I'll just have to work harder to earn her approval I guess," I say.

"But really. I *am* sorry to bug you," she says, her face wistful.

"There are other places in your apartment where you can cry." I lift both palms up.

An even bigger smile curves her lips as she rests her forearms on the railing of her balcony. "Well, what if I want to wallow on my bed with my Netflix and my tub of The Tonight Dough ice cream, huh? The couch is not going to work in this scenario."

I wince. "And what are you watching?"

"I have plans to watch some cheesy Christmas movies. But first, the 2005 version of *Pride and Prejudice*."

I whistle, and it sounds low and depressed, like I hoped it would. "Oh. Just like I thought. This is serious."

"You don't know *P and P*."

"I do, too," I counter. "My mom showed it to me once. It's not bad. But there's no way I'm sitting through the really long one from the nineties."

"This might be controversial, but there are parts of this Keira Knightly version that might be better anyway." She cringes and laughs, and I can see the condensation from her breath in the cold night air.

"Scandalous, dahling." I chuckle. "But seriously. A romantic movie and ice cream on your bed? What's up?"

She sighs and looks out into the dark sky. "For someone who doesn't have any sisters, you sure know the drill, don't you?"

"Camilla's a good teacher. Besides, my mom taught me stuff, too."

"I know." But it's clear Aria's snark isn't coming from my comment. Something much deeper is at play here, and I'm going to find out what happened if it kills me.

"Seriously, though," I continue. "Did a great-aunt die and leave her inheritance to her pet goldfish instead of you?"

She rolls her eyes and shakes her head. "I might as well tell you." She shoots me a glance and rubs her eyes. "Rob and I broke up."

I swear I hear angels singing out in the vast night as they float by on wispy, celestial clouds. But I can't start singing "Hallelujah" in front of her.

"Oh no. I'm sorry."

"It's okay," she shoots out. "It actually happened months ago."

I try not to let it bother me that she allowed me to believe they were still together. "Then why the . . ." I pause and make a circling motion around my head with a sniff of my nose and patting my eyes.

She snorts. "I heard some news that . . . I wasn't prepared for, I guess."

"So, what happened? I mean, did you tell him to jump off a cliff or was it the other way around?"

"Are you asking if I got dumped? Wow. Subtle, Theo."

"No. Well, okay, yes. I'm wondering how things went down. I can't help you as well if I don't know the deets." I'm tempted to rub my upper arms and stamp my feet back and forth to warm up. But there's no way I'm going to make her feel bad by thinking I'm too cold to be out here.

"I'm not going to be giving you any deets. Geez, Theo." She pauses and licks her lips, her eyelashes fluttering. "I'll summarize by saying he told me this spring that we need to either get engaged or break up." She shrugs. "I agreed and told him I needed some time. I guess I took too long to decide, which was a decision in and of itself. We officially broke up in September."

I weigh her words, letting the silence sink in around us. Finally, I catch her gaze. "I'm sorry. You two dated a long time. I'm sure it's hard."

She stares back. "Thanks."

"So what happened tonight to cause the ice cream and *P and P* sesh?"

"A social media post." She gives up a stilted laugh. "A photo of him with a woman with a ring on her finger."

"What? Already?"

"Yep. He wrote out their story. Apparently, the woman was living in Europe until she went to Arkansas to live with her brother the end of September. Her brother is Rob's good friend. And the rest is history. Things happened fast."

"That's crazy. I can't imagine making such a life-altering decision that fast."

"I know. Obviously, me neither. But they seem really happy. Good for each other, actually. I maybe did a little social media stalking of her accounts." She cringes and bites down on her bent pointer finger.

"I can see how that could be hard to find out, though," I offer.

"It hit me hard that he was ready for marriage. It wasn't an 'us' problem. It was a 'me' problem. I sort of feel broken." She raises her voice, leans heavily on the railing, and gestures with her hands. "He's brave enough to move forward and get married and what am I? Stuck. The thought of marriage is terrifying."

"I agree. But why do you feel that way?"

"Well, my parents. And my grandparents." She shakes her head bitterly. "My mom's always saying how charming my dad was until they got married. My dad says the same thing about her, too. I know they love each other, deep down. But all they can see is the hurt. The changes." She whisks a tear from her cheek with one quick swipe. "Anyway, I'm happy for Rob. I just feel sort of lame. Like I can't get it together. Like I'm a child almost."

There's nothing childish about this incredible woman, and I want to say that. But I don't know how to convey it properly.

She pins the blanket against her with one hand and then grabs her hair and starts raking through it with the other. It looks like it hurts, with the way she's pulling on it. "Also?" she adds. "I think I'm sad that I'm not sad, you know?"

"Uh . . ."

"Like, he was such a big part of my life for so long. Shouldn't I be in mourning right now? Shouldn't I feel stricken with grief that not only did we break up, but now he's marrying someone else?"

"I think it's handy you don't. Feeling sad sucks."

She gives a watery laugh. "I mean, yes and no. But what does that say about me?" She pulls a face and digs into her sweats pocket, bringing up a tissue to dab at her eyes. "That I hung onto a relationship that I don't care about for so long? Why have I done this?"

"All this stuff is above my paygrade. I'm not a therapist. But it's good to know he wasn't the one."

Her silence tells me maybe she agrees.

"Does Camilla know?" I finally ask.

Aria shakes her head. "About the breakup, yes. But not this. I didn't want to call her since I know she'd rush right over, but she's been helping me so much with moving and everything, I didn't want to take up more of her time."

"She'll actually want to kill me if she knew I knew before she did."

Aria giggles. "That's very true. I just don't want her to come over."

"Then tell her you're going to bed. Or tell her in the morning and I'll fake surprise."

A smile plays about her lips. "Show me your 'I had no idea Aria's ex got engaged so fast' face."

I give her my face of agony and shock—and in my mind it's a pretty good mash up of Edvard Munch's painting, "The Scream" and the scene from *The Princess Bride* when Westley gets hooked up to the torture machine.

"What? Do you think I'm a monster?" Her eyes well with tears and she disappears into her room.

"Wait, wait, sorry. I'm not good at this. Come back."

She returns in a moment with a fresh tissue.

"Here. How's this?" I give an exaggerated gasp and cover my mouth. I will my eyes to well with tears. "Aria, this is a shock."

"That's a little better, you big goof. Look, my head hurts. I should skip the movies and go to sleep. Except I'm kind of freaked out that you can hear me so well."

"I can't. You just happened to be crying really loudly."

She grunts. "I don't think so."

"In all honesty, it took me a while to know what was happening over there. And you didn't bother me. I'm glad you told me, Aria. And for what it's worth, *I* am sad you're sad." For some reason, the way she's looking at me, with those fawn-like brown eyes searching mine, emboldens me. "I'm not sorry you guys broke up. But I am sorry you're sad."

She only nods and quirks a brief smile before removing the blanket from her shoulders, balling it up, and throwing it to me. I catch it and the sweet strawberry scent of her is in the air. I resist the urge to press my nose to the blanket.

No promises I won't later.

She returns to her apartment, closing her door with a firm click.

I close mine, too, and then collapse in my chair, the warm blanket still in my hands.

Aria is single.

And that thought about taking her on one date just to say that I've done it—just to get her out of my system?

That was a bunch of bull. A hundred dates couldn't do that.

Chapter 16

Aria

After a tormented sleep where I dream of drinking hot cocoa clogged with marshmallows with my first-grade teacher and lamenting to her about my love life, or lack thereof, I get up and go into work, my eyes bloodshot.

It's odd, but something I didn't tell Theo last night was that the pervasive feeling I had when Rob and I broke up was *relief.*

Relief that it was over.

What kind of a person am I? This is probably why I dreamt of having a therapy session with Ms. Coombs. Life made so much more sense in first grade, didn't it?

And now that Rob's engaged? Maybe I'm jealous of his bravery . . . of his ability to jump wholeheartedly into something when he and I couldn't even manage to live in the same state for the majority of our relationship.

To top things off, I blabbed my issues to Theo on the balcony. My stomach plunges to my knees when I think of him hearing me cry through the wall. So embarrassing.

As soon as I arrive at the bakeshop in the cold of morning—don't let the brilliant sunshine fool you, it's freezing outside—Camilla grasps me by the shoulders.

"You look—" She shakes her head, her blond corkscrew curls bouncing from side to side. "What happened?" Her eyes are wide, and her gaze is whipping through me, assessing everything about me.

I take a minute to plop my wallet and keys in their spot on the shelf below the register. "Rob's engaged."

Camilla's still, silent for several seconds, the only movement coming from her rapidly blinking eyes. Then she steps forward and crushes me in a hug.

"That happened fast." She's shorter than me by a whole head, so her voice is buried in my dress. Yes, I'm wearing a dress to work, which was probably Camilla's first clue that something was off. It's not a nice dress. It's simply long, loose, and comfortable, and it has pockets. It's wash and wear, warm, and periwinkle, one of my best colors.

I pull away from her hug. "I'm fine. Truly."

She grimaces. "Was he cheating on you?"

"No. His fiancée had been living in Europe for years. They only met when she moved in with her brother, Rob's friend."

She tugs on my hand and drags me to one of the café-style tables we have in the front. Placing her hands on my shoulders, she forces me to sit and then takes the chair opposite of me. I notice she's put up her signature forest green and burgundy Christmas decorations all around the room.

"Well, I know this is a good thing," Camilla says. "But are you okay?"

I lick my lips and nod. It's actually sort of nice to be here in the bakeshop this morning—with the familiar black and white floor tiles and white cedar tables and chairs. It feels like home.

The thought of moving on, of finding a new job in brand management, fills me with dread.

"Yes. But do you remember how I felt relieved when we broke up?" I reach out to play with the silver ribbon on Camilla's holiday table centerpieces. "Right now, there's some weird guilt-sadness kind of a thing going on because I should probably be a lot more wrecked about this than I am. Rob and I were together for four years. We shouldn't have lasted that long, but we did. He's been with this woman for, like, two months." I knead my forehead with my fingers. "And it's not like I want him back or anything like that. I'm truly happy for him. I just wonder what all this says about me."

Camilla eyes me carefully. "Rob wasn't right for you. That's all." She claps her hands together once, her brows knitting together. "So, should we cyberstalk his new fiancée?"

"Ha! I already did. She seems like a lovely person." I stand from the table and jam my hands in my pockets. "I'll come help you in the kitchen, and we can talk while we work. You have a lot to do before the festival."

Once we're in the kitchen with our aprons on and ingredients out, Camilla pipes up. "The bright side is, at least you didn't marry Rob." She shivers. "We can all be thankful it never came to that. And I think instead of condemning yourself for not ending it a long time ago, give yourself some grace, Aria. There's a good reason for the things we do, right? I'm sure it was a form of protection." She waves me away. "I don't know. But the bottom-line is, today is the first day of the rest of your life."

I give her a warm smile. "That's so cliché, Camilla," I say.

"It is, but it's true! We need to celebrate."

"I'd settle for a quick meal with you."

"Tonight?" Camilla's smile beams.

"I wish, but I have the committee meeting. And we've already been warned this one will be long."

"Fine. But tomorrow night? Or this weekend? You're all mine." Camilla wiggles her fingers like she's a monster ready to attack. I can't help but laugh.

"You mentioned the festival," she says. "What's the latest with that?"

I don't miss the tone. She's talking about Theo, but she's too good of a friend to ask me that outright at this moment.

"Theo and I have to nail down some plans for the big dinner we're in charge of. I wonder how Carl and Amanda did all of this and still managed to report the news. It's a lot."

"I'm here to help." Camilla places a floured hand on my shoulder. "And Aria? If you need to take some time off to process, that's great. You do what you need to do."

"I'm fine."

Camilla presses her lips together tightly before responding. "Glad to hear it. But you don't have to be if you're not."

I laugh. "Relationally stunted? Terrified of marriage? Yeah. But I really am okay, I promise."

And I am. Thoughts of Theo warm me, much like the blanket he gave me last night. It was a kind gesture. All of it was kind.

I get to work on the cheesecakes. I've started making five large ones each day, which are sliced into twelve pieces each. But we sell out of them every day now, so today I set out to make six. Camilla and I bake while Danene, Merre, and Elijah mind the register and work on order fulfillment.

As I bake, thoughts of Theo infiltrate my mind. I remember him leaning on his railing in the dark, trying to hide the fact that he was getting cold. I was too, but a part of me didn't want our conversation to stop. I think he meant what he said, that he was sad for me. And that he wasn't sad that Rob and I broke up.

It's nearly noon when I'm finished. I grab a cheesecake for the bakery case and rotate my body around so I can open the swinging door.

The door stops prematurely just as I'm swiveling around to face the front. I smack into Theo's chest, and the platter of cheesecake smashes against his shirt in an oomph.

We both gasp, and, seeing the destruction all over Theo, Merre and Danene shriek.

"Oh, no! I'll get some paper towels," Merre says, pushing past us to get into the kitchen. Camilla soon joins us, and Elijah laughs as he takes the paper towels from Merre and hands them to us.

Theo looks down at the cheesecake plastered against him. I stare at the mess. I'm frozen, one hand glued to my mouth, the other holding the platter. I have no idea what to do with it now.

"I am so sorry," Theo says, peeling his shirt away from his skin. "I've ruined an entire cheesecake."

I clear my voice and find my words. "No, it was my fault. I should have looked where I was going." I gaze at the mess and my heart sinks. The cheesecake is toast, all eight pounds of it.

"Here, let me pay for it," he says, wiping off his hands on a clean corner of his shirt before reaching for his wallet in his back pocket.

Merre hems and haws before pressing the wad of paper towels to his chest. He sets a couple of twenties on the counter before grabbing the paper towels from her.

"Thanks, but paper towels aren't going to cut it. I'll call Jesse and have him bring me a new shirt. I don't have another client for forty-five minutes."

"I'll call him," Camilla says. "You go clean up." She glances at me. "Aria, help the poor man out."

"Here," I say, motioning to the back kitchen door. "There's a bathroom over there." We go past Camilla's office and into the next small room.

Theo's laugh reverberates against the walls of the tiny bathroom as he sees himself in the mirror. "I'm such a hot mess," he says in a southern accent.

This man and his accents. He fans his face and then tries to slide bits and pieces of the cheesecake off the fabric of his shirt. "I wanted this *in* my belly, not *on* my belly."

I laugh and reach out a finger. "I hadn't had a chance to taste it yet." There's a particularly heavy chunk and I swipe a bit of it off and lick my finger.

Theo watches me carefully. What am I doing? I turn to the sink and wash my hands, then as I'm drying them, I grab a bunch of extra paper towels and turn to face him. He's looking down at his shirt, peeling cheesecake off it and eating it, too.

"You don't have to do that. Here," I say and try to hand him the towels. I could wipe his chest down myself, but that seems inappropriate.

He shakes his head. "I'm eating as much of this as I can. It's amazing."

The back of my throat burns with pride. "Is that why you came? To get a slice?"

"I came to see how you were doing." He gives me a sideways glance. "How are you feeling today?"

"I'm fine," I wave him away. I think I really am fine. "We should discuss the big dinner."

His blue-eyed gaze takes me in a moment before he nods. "Right. We're supposed to have everything finalized by tonight, aren't we?"

He starts to unbutton his shirt and I snap my eyes shut. Then, realizing that's a tad immature, I open them again, but turn to the side so I can stare at the white wall.

"I really don't want to stand here any longer with half a cheesecake stuck to me," he says. "My shirt's absorbing it and I think it's seeping into my skin."

"Oh, yeah, yeah. Of course." I cross my arms in front of me and clear my throat. If I talk about the dinner, maybe my mind can be distracted from the fact that he's partially undressing right in front of me in the tiniest bathroom known to man. I can even feel his body heat emanating from him, his minty scent disarming me.

We go over the plans, discussing the catering company, the menu options, and when we'll need to arrive at Barrie Mansion the night of.

"And we're serving your cheesecake, right?"

"If you're not sick of it, now that you've been thoroughly bathed in it." I turn to him, but my laugh is snuffed out by the sight of his bare chest.

"Oh, now it's become one with my soul, Aria."

His stare shakes me to my core. I swallow hard.

"You and my cheesecake have just imprinted, huh?" I joke. "Are you soulmates?"

He sobers, his gaze boring into mine. "No. My soul needs something else. Someone else."

The way he's looking at me is not full of heat in the classic sense—in the "Theo is a Flirt" sense. It's raw, like he's not sure he should have said it, but it's out there, like it or not. He balls his shirt with both hands near his waist.

My gaze falters first, landing on his abs. He's so tall, his torso long and lithe, like a swimmer's. I look up at the ceiling.

"Well, I should leave you to it." My laugh sounds fake in my ears. "I don't know why I'm still standing here."

"We had to discuss the dinner. Sorry again about ruining a perfectly good cheesecake. And it *was* good, Aria."

I glance at his eyes for one beat before I look away again. I'm trying to remind myself of all the reasons why I can't feel this way when I'm around Theo. But it's hard to remember them.

"I'm sorry about getting it all over you. See you tonight," I say with a little wave, and I spin around to open the door. Must leave the presence of this attractive man right now before my whims and thoughts get the best of me and I say or do something stupid.

Jesse's there, on the other side of the door, his hand stretched out to open it, his other hand holding a hanger with a clean dress shirt.

He glances at me, then at Theo, then back at me, and his smile is crooked and smug.

Oh so smug.

Chapter 17

Theo

Aria's caught me staring at her twice in this committee meeting, and I utter a shaming reminder to myself to rein it in.

The woman's long-time boyfriend just got engaged to someone else. She needs space, and at the very most, a friend—and only a friend—to talk to.

Liz and Marjorie are presenting on the number of sponsors who have pulled out of the festival since the scandal hit. The tone is equal parts "We got this" and "Everybody panic!"

I glance around the room at the New Hedge Community Center. I can see why they have these mismatched recliners, and I'm surprised there's only one person falling asleep. It's the same guy every time, Newt Arniston. I think he's in his mid-eighties, though, so he has a good excuse.

I don't think I could fall asleep even if I wanted to because Aria is right next to me. Yes, we're in separate recliners, of course. But I could reach out and touch her. Every time she moves her right arm, her bracelets ring as they clash against each other, gold and silver bangles that slide along her wrist in a stupidly mesmerizing way.

We introduce plans for the dinner coming up in less than a week. Aria wants to do complex table settings, and she's brought some mockup designs. As I get ready to turn the time over to her, I feel slightly out of my league.

"If it were up to me, I'd order in a huge batch of wings and rolls and get some big screens up with the football games, but Aria vetoed that idea." The room erupts in laughter, more than I deserve. "So, take it away, Aria."

I sit back down and look over at her. I can't decide if her dress is a light blue or light purple, but either way, she looks good in it. She rises from the recliner, somehow looking elegant. I think she's the only person I've ever known to look graceful while getting out of a recliner.

"It's true, he did mention a wings-and-football theme." She tosses an amused glance at me, and for a second, I'm rendered useless, caught up in everything about her.

Which isn't good or fair to her. She just got out of a serious, long relationship. I can't be that guy. I can't be the rebound.

In any other situation in the past, if a woman was looking for a rebound to ease her emotional pain, and we both knew what the expectations were, then sure, I'd date her.

But Aria? Aria's different.

Besides, I keep reminding myself that she didn't actually just break up. It's been a couple of months. All that time and she didn't say anything to me—keeping her distance under the guise of being in a relationship. That probably tells me a lot about where her feelings are for me . . . or at least it should.

But I keep thinking about last night on our balconies. If they were a foot or two closer together, nothing would have been able to stop me from jumping into hers and wrapping her in a hug. And not because I was cold.

She gives a short slide presentation to the board about the caterers, menu, and place settings. I can't help beaming with pride at the smiles of the committee members as she wraps up. Even Newt is awake now and semi-alert.

I don't blame him. It's Aria. She could make a sloth feel alive enough to run a 50-meter race.

Marjorie stands next. "That all sounds fantastic. Make sure the purchase orders are turned in to the accounting people in advance." She gestures to two people in recliners in the far corner. "If you have any questions on how to do that, just ask."

Then the meeting is turned over to Liz, and she talks about how they've been measuring the success of the marketing campaign. "Our golden couple here is hitting it out of the park! Everyone loves the chemistry. I don't want to make any rash predictions or anything like that, but if these numbers are to be believed, we might get our best turnout we've ever had." Her face falls. "If we can get our sponsorships back."

Aria flicks a glance at me, and nerves show on her face.

"Okay," I whisper to her. "No pressure, right?"

Her brows go up and she tilts her head in concession, as if to say, *Thems the breaks.* Still, there's an underlying sadness in her expression.

The rest of the meeting, I'm taking notes and trying not to get distracted by Aria. But there's one pervasive thought that's pulsing in my head over and over again.

She's single. She's single. She's single.

"You still tasting the cheesecake bath?" Aria asks me as we head out to our cars. It's nine o'clock and the meeting has ended. We're puffing out condensation with every breath.

"I had to spritz cologne all over me, even with the new shirt Jesse brought me. And then I took a shower when I got home from work."

She shakes her head and laughs. "I still can't believe you got plastered with cheesecake."

"Speaking of the bakeshop, I have to go over to my office and get some things. The big pro bono case is coming up."

"Okay, well, I might see you over there," she says, before hurrying into her car.

Just because my office is right next to her bedroom doesn't mean I have to see her. I shouldn't. I have work to do and not much time to do it.

But when I reach my office and grab my files, I'm not sure where my head's at. I could check to make sure she's okay. She wasn't okay last night, and I'm glad I was able to help her not be so alone.

I should probably check on her real fast.

I can hear her move around in her bedroom. I screw up my face in apprehension before deciding to go for it.

"Knock, knock," I shout through the wall.

"Hey Theo," she shouts back.

"I wanted to check on how you're doing."

There's a long pause and I'm about to repeat myself when I hear her say. "Can I come over to your office? For just a minute?"

Every emotion under the sun shifts through me. "Uh. Sure." I start throwing papers and files around to tidy up. "I'll let you in in like, one minute?"

"Make it two," she says, and I hear her footsteps leaving her bedroom.

She's still in her dress when I open the office's main doors downstairs.

"Come on in," I say, nervous that I've got a single Aria in my midst and we're alone in the office.

I'm pretty sure Weatherby has security cameras set up in here. I know he did in the old place.

There. That thought alone will keep me from making choices with Aria that I should not make.

Charlotte, the receptionist, has decorated for Christmas with pre-lit birch trees, pinecone garlands, and starry curtain lights. The ambiance is kind of nice—which is hard for a Christmas-hater like myself to say.

But maybe I hate Christmas a little bit less this year with so much of Aria in it.

"Can we sit here?" She motions to the seating area.

I'm relieved we're not going up to my office. There's a tension in the air, and I can't figure out what it is.

"Sure," I motion to the sofas. "Have a seat." I rush over to the drink refrigerator behind the reception desk and grab us some water bottles. "And we have playing cards in the side table. Jay sometimes plays solitaire out here when he needs to think."

She settles onto the sofa and thanks me as she takes the bottle. "I'm so glad there's been a good response to the advertising for the festival."

"Yeah, me too." I sit across from her. "And everyone seemed to like our ideas for the dinner."

She nods and traps her bottom lip between her teeth.

Have mercy. Anything to do with her mouth is going to be the death of me.

"I hope it's enough to convince the sponsors to come back," she says.

"It will be." I'm optimistic. The festival is an institution. This one thing isn't going to bring the whole thing down. "So? How have you been feeling today?" I ask. "For real? Now that we don't have an audience."

"And now that you're not covered in cheesecake," she adds with a laugh.

"Exactly." I chuckle.

"I'm feeling well. I know it was the right decision for us to break up, I've never doubted that. And I wish them the best." She sighs and massages her temples. "I actually have a question for you, though."

"Oh really?"

She nods and releases a breath. "Why do you hate Christmas?" She holds up a hand. "Is it the elves? Or did Santa bring you a lump of coal?" She laughs, and when I don't smile her eyes widen. "Oh. Was that it?"

I shake my head, feeling hot under the collar. "It's not a huge deal. I've never been a fan, that's all."

Her smile is cautious. Warm. "Even as a kid? Now I'm sad for you." She shrugs. "You can tell me. I opened up to you last night. Your secrets are safe with me."

"Why do you want to know?" I feel it welling up inside of me, this need to tell her, this need to shout it to the world that what happened was not cool.

"We're supposed to be these big advocates for Christmas." She slides her hands into her dress pockets. "I worry that this is asking too much of you."

"I can go along with it. It's for a good cause. I hate that the kids who needed shoes and their extracurriculars paid for didn't get that, so I want to help."

"Me, too."

We're quiet for a while before she looks back at me. "I feel like if the festival goes away, I'll lose the only truly happy thing of my childhood Christmases," she says.

"How so?"

"My grandpa. He was the one to take us. He spoiled us there, buying us crap we didn't need. We were so happy. That's why the festival is so important to me."

"Well, that and the blazer," I add with a smile.

"Of course. It's the most powerful of all power suits."

I drop my head back in a laugh. "And Aria? This might sound strange, but it's what I'm feeling, so I'm just going to say it." I claw at the stubble on my chin, too short to be called a beard. But right now, it's giving me courage I don't normally have. "Hearing about why the festival is important to you makes me want to do everything in my power to make sure it happens," I say. "Like I want to fight like a dragon for it."

"Thank you, Theo. Sometimes I feel optimistic about it. Other times not so much. But knowing you care? That means a lot."

I decide to go for it. I have nothing to lose. "My dad left on Christmas Eve. He made an effort to be there while we opened presents, and then he told us he was moving out. And he did."

Aria's quiet for several seconds, her eyes soft. "Oh, that's horrible." Her voice is raw. "I'm sorry, Theo."

I nod. "I feel bad my mom had to go through that. I was five, and I didn't understand fully what was going on. But of course she did. And Jesse was eight. He had a hard time."

"No wonder this time of year is difficult. It brings back so many haunting things."

"Yeah. And I know that's not what the holiday is all about. But it is a reminder of the bad stuff."

We're quiet and I try to block out images and scents and sounds from my memory.

She stands and joins me on my sofa, sitting close enough to reach out and place a hand over mine. I feel its soft warmth. "If there's ever anything I can do to help, please tell me. If there's something triggering, I can take care of it for you."

"I appreciate that." I need to change the subject. "And what about you? I've never had an ex get engaged around the holidays."

She giggles. "I thought you didn't date one person long enough to have exes. Have you ever even been dumped before?"

She removes her hand from mine, and I'm disappointed.

"I've been dissed. Does that count? I've been forgotten about. But dumped? Dumped would necessitate a relationship to speak of.

And I've never had that." Shame wells up in me. I'm nearing my late twenties. Shouldn't I have had a relationship or two by now?

"Well, that's good. I'm glad you've never been dumped."

But there's something in her expression, a hesitation. She even pulls back and away from me.

"Look," I say. "It's good I've never been dumped, but I don't like that I've never dated anyone seriously," I tell her. "It says a lot that you can commit to one person for years. I admire that."

"Well, maybe it would have been better if I hadn't. I knew I didn't feel for him the way I should have. But it was easy and safe." She squeezes her lips tightly together.

I want her to go on, to tell me more. But I don't know if she will—if she feels comfortable opening up. Still, I can't help myself.

"And easy and safe was appealing to you? Why?"

She shakes her head. "I don't know." It's a dismissal. She doesn't want to talk about this anymore, and I have to respect that.

"Want to play cards?" I ask.

"You have work to do." She moves to get up.

I reach out a hand. "But it's you . . ." I stop myself, even though it's true. I'll work all night long if that means I get to spend more time with her now.

"Okay. Only if I choose the game." A slight smile skates across her face.

I grin back and reach over to the drawer in the side table. I open it and pull out a pack of playing cards.

"These cards are handy in a pinch." I slide the deck out of the box.

"And right now is a pinch?"

"Right now, it's a necessity." I shuffle, enjoying the feel of the cards on my thumbs. I can't resist doing a couple of tricks with the deck. I learned a thing or two with cards in college. I know it's showing off a little. "What are we playing?"

She doesn't seem impressed with my skills, but for some reason, that only makes me want to try harder. For what or to gain what, I don't know.

"The game is called Toenails," she announces, grabbing the cards from my hand. She sounds a little like a bored Vegas card dealer. She rotates to face me, sits cross-legged, bunches up her dress so it's out of the way, and leans forward so the long couch cushion can act as a table for the cards. She spreads them out face up, rearranging them as she tells me the rules.

It seems simple enough, if not a little addictive. We start the game and every time something happens in my favor, she gives up a yelp or a snicker.

"You're just bummed that I'm so naturally gifted at this game," I say, after she screams a long and tortured "Noooooo!" when I go up several points.

"It's ninety-five percent luck, Theo."

"Well, that last five percent, that's all me, baby."

She giggles and hiccups and smacks her mouth with both hands. I laugh and she throws her head back, her gaze on the ceiling.

"I never lose at this game," she says with an over-the-top whine.

"Oh, I get why you wanted to play it."

"It's not that. It's my favorite."

"But you want to beat me so bad you can taste it."

"Yeah. And it's fun to see your tells." She challenges me with a look.

"My tells?"

"You sniff right before you lay down a good card."

"I do? Man. No wonder I'm terrible at poker."

"If you're terrible at poker, it's only because your face is so animated that it's clear what you're thinking every second. You can't hide anything."

"Really? You think you know what I'm thinking?" I try to keep a neutral face, but Aria's grinning so hard that I start to smile, too.

She studies me. "You're regretting the burrito you ate for dinner," she says, moving to poke my stomach with her finger.

I capture her finger before she reaches me. "I didn't eat a burrito for dinner. I had a sensible salad," I insist. "And okay, a few slices of bread."

"Fine. You're thinking this is the greatest game known to man."

I shrug. "Okay. I'll give you that."

"And you're also feeling scared that I'll win."

"I'm way up. I'm not scared I'll lose." Releasing her hand, I grow serious and clear my throat. "What else am I thinking?"

She puckers her lips. Not to kiss, of course, but because she's deep in thought. That doesn't mean I don't think about what it would be like to kiss her. For a very long while.

"That this has turned out to be a really great night? That's what I'm thinking, anyway." She ducks her head, running a finger along the fabric of the sofa.

"Nice powers of deduction, Aria. That's exactly what I was thinking."

"Thank you for helping me not feel so alone," she says.

"Well, thank you for understanding why Christmas is hard."

An hour passes and we each win two rounds. With a laugh, she stands.

"I'd better go."

"What? You're leaving on a tie breaker?"

Her eyes sparkle. "Well, we'll just have to break the tie another time."

"I'm okay with that," I say with a nod.

She studies the floor. "Thanks," she says before reaching her arms out for a hug. I wrap my own around her, relishing the feeling of her pressed against me.

She's heaven. My carefully constructed platonic goals are rapidly crumbling. She smells like sugared strawberries, her body precious in my arms. She shudders, almost imperceptibly, and those goals are dust between my fingers.

I drop my head enough that my mouth is inches from her neck. I see the powdered dust of freckles across her nose. Her glossy, dark mane has moved away from her neck enough that it would be so simple, so natural to press a kiss there. With another sigh, she leans her temple close to me, and I wonder if she can feel my breath against her skin. Does she want me to kiss her? Her temple, her cheek are right there, ready for the taking, for the feasting.

I've long admired the planes of her face, her ballerina posture, and now? It's so close. Does she want this?

An image of Rob comes to mind, which is ridiculous because I've never even met the man. I've only seen the one picture. But in my minds' eye—my crazy, not thinking straight mind's eye—he's missing a couple of teeth and has a truly terrible mullet.

I can't do this. There's no way I'll be the rebound. There's no way I'll even take that risk right now. Aria deserves more.

I pull away and the look of sadness in her eyes almost makes me snatch her back in my arms and kiss her.

Almost.

Chapter 18

Aria

A dash of disappointment that Theo has pulled away hits my insides and creeps out and along my limbs.

I lift those limbs—my arms at least—to his shoulders. But this time, I coil them around to the back of his neck and press my hands against his lat muscles.

He has flecks of gold in his bluer-than-blue eyes.

Wait. Flecks of gold and pinpoints of woodsy brown. What kind of a world do those eyes belong in?

A world of fairy dust and magic—of crystal springs and beckoning blue skies peeking through wooded canopies. I'd like to live there and explore every inch of that world.

Awash in sensations I've never known, I peck his lips.

Once. Only a dab of a kiss.

But it's enough to spread warmth throughout my body, a skittering of goosebumps against the rush of heat.

I have to have more, so I brush my lips against his again. And again, the sensations of craving, of adoring, of appreciating everything about him flow through me.

He responds, his lips pressing firmly against mine, a grunt of surprise and something like happiness rumbling deep inside his chest.

The faint scent of mint, mixed with the essence of evergreen spice is in my nose. The warmth of his mouth is on my lips. And for only a moment, I live in it. Enjoy it. Tangle it around my memory so I never lose it.

I take a step back, still dizzy from my lips on his.

And I laugh, a gurgle of shock—both from my kissing him and from the way it upended me.

"Thanks again for the cards and the distraction. I'd better get back to my apartment." I'm talking more rapidly with every word I say. "I haven't even figured out what to buy for my family. And Camilla's always so good at giving gifts, so I can't just show up on Christmas day with a gift card or bag of candy, can I?"

I take a breath and it's too scary to look him in the eyes, so I start talking again as I head for the glass double doors. "Not that I don't like candy for Christmas, but I should probably give out something more meaningful, right? I love caramel at Christmastime, though. Those chocolate caramel turtles at that candy store in the mall? Insane!"

I pull at the collar of my dress. "In fact, I'm thinking about making a caramel turtle cheesecake, which I'm guessing would sell really well."

I reach the door. I open it, needing to be free of my awkward words. Already, the uncertainties surrounding that kiss have parched my mouth. I clear my throat.

"Uh, have a good night." The sound of my own erratic drum of a heartbeat is so loud that when I can hear Theo tell me to wait, I'm surprised. I turn around, standing in the open doorway. I force myself to look at him—really look at him since I kissed him.

His mouth is a little slack, his eyes are searing into mine, like he wants to understand everything about me. Or at least my actions of the last thirty seconds or so.

"You okay?" Theo's voice is lower than I've ever heard. He's reached the first door, and I'm at the second, exterior one.

I give one quick shake of my head. "I'm sorry. I wasn't thinking."

Not waiting for a response, I hurry outside and next door to Shorty's, fumbling with the keys in the cold air until I take a breath and slow down enough that I can get inside. I let out a frustrated grunt once I'm in and then another one when the door's closed and I'm heading up the stairs to my new place.

I kissed Theo Carter.

I'm emotional since my ex got engaged so quickly. That's why I kissed him.

I kissed Theo Carter?

It was merely my misguided search for a momentary pleasure to ease the heaviness of life.

Right?

No. That's not it. I know this.

With the thickness of desire and confusion still coursing through me, I make myself some chamomile and vanilla tea, willing it to calm me down.

Hugging an attractive, fun guy like Theo would have me feeling things I shouldn't feel. And the kiss? It was a simple, parting gesture, like a quiet handshake. In some European countries, with all their abrazos and whatnot, it would have meant nothing at all.

It didn't mean anything at all.

I don't think.

I drop my head back in a sigh. Why doesn't my brain listen to me when I tell it to stop thinking about Theo?

I sip my tea in my dimly lit kitchen, play stupid games on my phone, and audibly tell myself "no" every time I remember the way Theo's eyes lit up when he made a good move in the game, how his torso looked without his shirt on in the bakeshop bathroom, and the warmth of his lips on mine.

And I absolutely do not wonder if he's still in his office when I quietly go to bed. I even turn on my white noise app to make sure I don't hear anything, just in case.

With the clarity that only a cold November morning can bring, I'm awake before dawn, working on graphic designs for the festival. The work is challenging and enjoyable, and my head's still foggy from last night, so I'm not being held hostage by my own thoughts and regrets like I was before.

It was only a quick kiss to say goodbye.

And now it's time to hustle. I want a new job in brand management, and I've been perusing the online job boards like a gaggle of teen girls stalking some cute boys at the mall. Feeling a little nerdy, a little imposter syndrome-ish, and a lot like I have an unrequited crush, my finger has hovered over the "apply now" button. Except, I can't take the plunge. Yet.

And I *will* make this year's Charles Dickens Christmas Festival a smashing success.

Theo and I will save the festival if it kills us!

I make my six cheesecakes, and the familiarity of the task calms me. The measuring, the mixing, the crushing, the baking. All is right in the world when I can make cheesecake.

Danene leaves, the smell of fresh bread in her wake. Merre is on her break, and Elijah's on a delivery run. I corner Camilla in the kitchen, up to her eyeballs with shortbread.

"I have something to tell you because I can't not tell you and have it fester and stew between us." I screw my eyes shut, bracing myself.

She raises one eyebrow. "Oh? What's going on?"

"It's nothing." I laugh. "But we're always honest with each other, right?"

"Yes, we are." Camilla says. She sets her baking sheet on the stainless-steel countertop. She's an open person, and I owe her the same, even if it's regarding her brother-in-law.

"I did something last night, sort of . . ." I trail off, massaging the back of my neck. "And I'm only telling you this not because it's a big deal or because it's something that will continue, but because we're honest with each other and it's bugging me, and I have to get it off my chest."

"Spit it out!" Camilla cries.

I turn to face her. "Okay, okay. In full rebound mode, I gave Theo a teensy tiny kiss."

"On the lips?" Camilla gives an enquiring smile. Her eyes are blinking as though she's had a dark hood over them and I've just ripped it off in a bright room.

My gaze darts to the floor. I don't even have to say yes. She can read my mind like it's the back of a box of her favorite cereal.

I look up and Camilla's face shows every emotion possible, from surprise to concern. It lands on contentment, a sense of delight.

"Oh really?" She draws out the word and leans back on the countertop, her smile lazy.

I glance behind me and move in closer, lowering my voice. "Elijah and Merre could be back soon, so I don't know how much I can tell you right now." I shake my head to clear it. "It was almost nothing. I was feeling vulnerable. And a bit like an idiot that my ex got engaged so fast and I'd allowed us to stagnate for so long."

I shoot out a sigh. "Lots of thoughts going on about that whole thing. And after the meeting last night, I could hear him in his office and he knocked on the wall, and we talked through it, and I invited myself over to the firm." I squeeze her arm. "But we just stayed in the lobby and played a game."

She slaps her forehead. "There's so much in the words you just said, I don't know where to begin." She pauses, still grinning like it's Christmas morning. "You can hear each other through your shared wall?"

"Sometimes. We sort of have to shout to understand. But it's kind of handy."

"That's actually adorable."

"It's . . . whatever. But listen. After the card game, we stood up, I gave him a hug, he pulled away, but I—." I bunch my lips together, embarrassment hitting me like it just barely happened. "I grabbed him and planted one on him." I squeeze my eyes shut tightly; a year of my life being taken off because of the humiliation of it all.

"But it was short and sweet and . . ." Unbidden, my lips curve into a smile. "Soft. It was nice." I blink rapidly. "But it was nothing. And I'm hoping by getting it off my chest, by telling you, I won't need to discuss it with him. Ever."

"Theo's a very attractive man."

I throw my hands in the air and spin away from her. "You're not helping."

"I'm just saying, I don't fault you for your impetuous decision."

"I was feeling out of sorts." I give a firm shake of my head. "And Theo can be really nice. We had so much fun playing cards." I hold up my hands in surrender. "It was only the quickest of reboundiest kisses."

Camilla giggles. "We sound like we're in junior high, you know this, right?"

"Junior high?" Merre has returned from her break, and she pushes through the swinging doors of the kitchen carrying a bag of baby carrots and a bottle of juice.

Camilla looks at me, waiting for me to respond. She knows to not say anything. Although Merre probably wouldn't judge me for it if we told her.

"Camilla and I often revert back to our junior high days," I say. "It can be embarrassing sometimes."

"But it can also be fun," Camilla counters.

Merre takes a drink of juice before stowing it and the carrots in the fridge. She adjusts her turban back over her thick, toffee-colored hair, which she has to braid in two pieces to get it to stay inside the covering. "I sort of wish I was still in contact with my junior high friends. I think I liked it more than high school, if you can believe that."

"You grew up in Texas, right?" I ask.

She nods, but a frown crosses her features before she shrugs. "After I graduated high school, I left Plano for good. Had to get out of there. Been living in Colorado ever since."

"You didn't like Plano?" Camilla asks.

"No, I loved it," Merre insists. "My family's still there. It was the circumstances at the time." Her tongue darts out to moisten her lips. "Anyway, you do not want to hear my sob story, so I'll spare you. But like I was saying, junior high was actually really fun for me. Good memories."

"You're probably in the minority with that sentiment, Merre, but I'm happy for you." I tell her. "And I'm happy you're here working at Shorty's with us."

"Aw. Thanks. Me, too. I'm almost done with my pastry certificate in Denver, and then I'm hoping I can take some of the baking off Camilla's hands." She raises her brows and looks at Camilla expectantly. We knew when we hired Merre that she had the potential to be a real asset to the shop with her experience.

Which should help me feel better about leaving.

We're saved from any talk about why we were feeling particularly junior high-ish as Camilla and Merre have a lengthy discussion about pastry arts and the program she's in.

Just because we're no longer talking about Theo doesn't mean I'm not thinking of him. The truth is, I don't remember feeling this giddy over a guy *since* junior high. Sure, there was Rob. But it wasn't an exciting, soaring feeling to be dating Rob. It was borne of feeling stable, that getting into a relationship was the next logical step.

And that's what's so scary. I know if Theo and I had continued to kiss, or if we kiss again, things wouldn't be logical or stable or safe. If we kiss again, my world will never be the same.

Because Theo? Theo has the ability to wreck me, mind, body, and soul.

Chapter 19

Theo

"The caterers said they were throwing in a couple of additional side dishes for free," Aria says, tapping the pen she's holding on the notebook in front of her. "They said they want to do their part to help the festival."

"That's cool of them." I get distracted by Aria's mouth, especially when she presses the capped end of the pen to her chin as she concentrates.

We haven't discussed the kiss. We can't. We're sitting in the bakeshop at one of the tables and customers are coming in and out. Not to mention Merre and Elijah, who, between the two of them, haven't left us alone.

That's probably a good thing. But still, I want to talk with her about it. She apologized for it as she was leaving, and I want to make it very clear to her that no apology is necessary.

That kiss.

I shudder internally as it comes to mind again. There are some things in life that are innate, so impossibly simple that they make sense and there's no way to describe why they make so much sense.

Kissing Aria was like that for me. So tortuously brief, yet the single most powerful kiss I've ever had. Aria truly is on a different plane than others. And her kiss was no different.

The bell over the door rings. Aria leans her body to one side to see. "Grandpa!"

I turn to see a man with grey hair, bundled up in a coat, scarf, beanie, and gloves, stamping his feet to get the snow off them.

Aria stands and rushes to him. She's wearing a white sweater with tiny red bells sewn on, so it makes a slight jingle wherever she goes. I wouldn't think something like that would work, and it's Christmassy, so that's usually doubly annoying for me. But she makes it attractive—stick-in-your-mind-for-all-time attractive.

She gives him a big hug and then squeals and darts away. "Snow in my face? Grandpa!" She wipes her cheek off and turns to me, pointing to him. "This guy. A few days in Colorado and already he thinks he can stick snow in my face."

"I couldn't help myself. I'm finding snow in *all* the nooks and crannies these days."

"That snow was from a nook or a cranny?" Aria scowls and wipes her face again.

"The nooks and crannies of my coat, Aria." Her grandfather laughs. "My *coat*."

"Um hmm." Aria shakes her head, but tugs on his arm to bring him over to the table. I stand and reach out to shake his hand.

"Grandpa, this is Theo Carter. He works next door. He's an attorney and Camilla's brother-in-law." She turns to me. "And this is Howard Beckwith. The best grandpa in the universe."

"I'm the only grandpa she's ever known, so—" Howard lifts his hands in the air, palms up. "Still, I'm not too shabby if I do say so myself."

"Grandpa's getting used to the snow since he's lived in Florida for the last ten years."

"I can't get enough of it! I made a bunch of snow angels in the yard the other day," he says to me. "My daughter Erin, Aria's mom, wasn't too happy. She said I could have injured myself. The nerve!" His laugh is a booming, old-man-full-of-wisdom chuckle I didn't expect from someone so slight. It twitches his mustache, and I notice his eyes are the same shade of brown as Aria's.

She directs him to the display case. "Look, Grandpa. You're famous. It's your cheesecakes!"

"They look like they belong in a swanky Manhattan eatery," Howard says. "Good work, Aria."

He sits at the table next to ours, looking over at Aria's pad of paper. "Don't let me interrupt anything, you two. I thought I'd come see the shop. I haven't been since I was last here two years ago." He looks around the room and whistles. "I see the remodel is all finished. It looks mighty spiffy."

"Camilla did a good job, didn't she? And hey, you can thank me for the paint in here because I spent many a day with a long roller above my head. My hair was sticky with paint for weeks."

"Very nice," Howard takes in the paint before turning his attention back to Aria. "You outdid yourself. It looks professionally done."

"Grandpa believes in me when no one else does," Aria says. She laughs and reaches over to squeeze his shoulder. But there's a softening sadness in her expression. "It will be hard to leave this place when I find a new job, someday."

"But think of the rewards," Howard counters, his hands going wide. "It'll be a good move for you to branch out and do what you love."

She shrugs. "Maybe. Probably. We're going to the festival when it opens, right, Grandpa?"

"It wouldn't be Christmas without that." He gives her a glinting smile before turning his attention to me. "Now Theo, tell me about your work in the law. And then I'll tell you some of the finest lawyer jokes you've ever heard."

The squeak of the sneakers and basketballs at the New Hedge Rec Center is like the sound of a bell to Pavlov's dogs. Instant calm. Instant fun.

And it mostly shuts out thoughts of Aria's kiss last night.

It was a kiss unlike any I've ever had. Way too short. But holding so much intensity that, even now, I'm reduced to mush at the memory of it.

The problem is, it was a reaction to her sadness—and whatever else she was feeling about her ex getting engaged. Which is why it can't happen again.

Still. I'm frustrated she and I haven't had a chance to talk about it, even though it was fun spending time with her and her grandfather at the bakeshop today. Those two are something else together.

Here, at the rec, I'm playing one-on-one basketball against my brother Jesse, which makes everything better. I love to beat him at the game he taught me to play, but usually that only happens because I'm taller and have younger arms and legs.

But I can pretend I'm beating him because I'm that much better.

We take a quick break to get in line at the drinking fountain.

Jesse is in front of me—old men drink first—and he lifts the neckline of his T-shirt up to his face to wipe the sweat off.

"You need one of these," I tell him, lifting my new workout towel from my shoulder. No chafing against the skin, this thing is as smooth as butter and highly absorbent.

"Let me use it." He reaches for it.

"You cannot use my sweat towel." I lift it from my shoulder and hold it high in the air.

He doesn't play this game, instead waving me away. "You need a nice, specialized towel to impress the ladies here. The only woman I care about impressing had to work late to get things squared away for her booth at the festival. I've been meaning to ask, how is this year's co-host gig? Do not let my wife down by ruining the festival, you hear?" It's his turn in line, so he bends to get a drink.

I wait for him to finish at the water fountain before I respond. "Camilla will love this year's festival."

"I'm just glad our days of painting a booth are over," he says. "It's nice to have one that's still in good shape."

Jesse has moved to the side, so I lean over to take a long drag from the fountain.

"Speaking of impressing the ladies, what's happening with Aria?" he asks.

I start to choke on the water and cough a little. Another drink calms my throat and lungs down. I wipe my mouth with the towel, and we walk away from the drinking fountain. "Wow, you really went for it, didn't you?"

Jesse smirks at me. I'm guessing this line of questioning is payback for all the times I bugged him about Camilla before they got married.

"Did Camilla put you up to this? Because Aria and I are friends. That's it." I begin heading back to the basketball court.

"I saw you in the bathroom of Shorty's when I brought you a shirt." He stares at me long and hard, and I look away, bouncing the ball as I walk.

"Nothing happened in the bathroom, Jesse." I shake my head. Wild imagination much?

Except, there was a lot happening in that bathroom, it just wasn't the physical version. But the feelings? Yeah, there was a lot happening.

I'm also trying very hard not to think of the kiss—it was way too short, but it's burned in my brain forever. And it's getting harder and harder to explain away.

Jesse nods at my words, but his smile tells me he's not exactly buying it. "I know the power of Shorty's bakeshop, and the small spaces. Did I ever tell you about the time Camilla and I were kissing on a yoga ball and her Grammy came waltzing in?" Jesse drops his head back and laughs. "Let me just say, I did not handle it well. I ran away instead of dealing with her line of questioning."

"Okay, but I don't need to hear any more. I need to focus on schooling you in B-ball, my bro."

He shakes his head, but he doesn't have a comeback to my banter. "Seriously, Aria's a really great person."

"I know." I bring my leg up behind me to stretch my hamstring. "She's processing a lot of stuff, though."

"That's it? You can give it some time, you know. Or are you not patient enough?"

I grab the basketball at my feet and dribble it down the court. And there's no question I'm going to make a beeline for the exit the second this game is over.

I am patient enough. She's worth every ounce of patience I can muster.

I walk out the doors of the rec center, trying to hurry home so Jesse won't bug me again about Aria or gloat about beating me, when I hold the door open for a guy who works at Shorty's.

"Hey, it's the delivery guy for Shorty's Bakeshop!"

He stops and eyes me curiously. "Yeah. Hey." He's guarded, suspicious.

"I'm Theo. I work next door, so I've seen you around."

He nods and narrows his eyes, looking me up and down. Because I'm a glutton for punishment, and probably because I want to relish in anything and everything that even remotely has to do with Aria, I keep talking. "How are you liking the job, Elijah?"

He nods and then bunches up his mouth before answering. "I like it. I need more hours, though."

"Business is booming, so hopefully they can start giving you more to do soon."

He nods. "Hope so." With his tight expression and slump of his shoulders, it seems the poor kid has the weight of the world on his shoulders.

"Well, I guess we'll see you around," I say.

I like interacting with people when I'm out and about. There's something kind of nice about connecting with strangers on an elevator, or in this case, coming and going from the rec. And with Elijah, I'm glad I did. It seemed like he needed some kindness.

But I don't put two and two together until I sit down at home with my dog, Moose. It's over a bowl of Froot Loops, my computer open to a program with details on my caseload, that I start connecting the dots.

I'm shocked.

Chapter 20

Aria

I'm working in the bakeshop and thanks to Camilla and her obsession with playing that Justin Bieber song about mistletoe on repeat, I've got all things Theo on the brain. She's defending her decision because she's in love with her husband Jesse, so she's drawn to all those sweet, mushy songs. Also, the song has the word that sounds like "shorty," so she says it's our store's anthem.

In a few short hours, Theo and I will be co-hosting the big VIP dinner, and despite getting a million little things ready here and there throughout the day, the prevailing thought on my brain is about Theo himself.

I haven't seen him in a few days, and as idiotic as it sounds, I've sort of missed him.

Not in an "I Love You" sort of way, but in an "I'd Love to Hang Out Together" sort of way.

But it's good that we haven't seen each other. First and foremost, I don't want to hazard the possibility that he'll bring up the kiss. And our strictly business texts about the VIP dinner leave no room for dalliance into discussions of other things.

Other things. Like feelings and rebound kisses.

But also, I've been putting in extra hours on my design and branding work before and after my time at Shorty's, and it feels nice crossing things off my to-do list and helping the festival in any way I can.

I don't love that I don't know exactly what I'll do in my future. I know I need to move on—to spend my time doing what will fill me up long term.

But Shorty's is like my bubblegum pink, puffy coat on a cold Colorado day: protective, warm, secure. I'm not sure I'm ready to try to cut it out there in the big, bad, real world.

When Theo walks into the bakeshop right before I'm off at five, I get a thrill up and down my spine. It's like a zipper being zipped up and then unzipped.

Whip!

Whirl.

Wheee!

I'm not prepared for that reaction. And though it's thrilling and feels good—it's great to feel something besides regret or the million other things that come with a breakup and a rebound kiss—I don't know what to do with it.

Theo has a shy smile as he gazes at the floor, scuffing his shoe along it.

What? Theo, shy? This is too much, and I pause, wiping down the mint green display case to give him a grin.

"Well, hello," I say. I don't mean it to sound flirtatious, but it probably does. I'm so glad Danene's gone home, Camilla and Merre are in the kitchen, and Elijah's at the post office with today's mailings.

"How've you been?" He approaches the counter, his closely trimmed, barely-there facial hair drawing attention to his strong jaw, and his hair, glossy and the perfect shade of dark brown, almost falling over one eye.

Almost. Which is so picture perfect I have to squeal a little inside.

Hopefully I didn't squeal aloud.

"I've been great. And you?"

Please don't mention the kiss.

I'm saying this to both of us. Internally only, of course. Because it felt like, the other day, we were seconds away from a disastrous bringing up of The Kissing Event of the Year. Like the subject was on the tips of our tongues.

Great. Now I'm thinking of Theo's tongue.

"Better now." He lets out a big sigh. "I see you've been doing your magic with the cheesecakes." He indicates the white boxes and Styrofoam sauce containers on the butcher block behind me.

I toss a glance back at the boxes. "They're cool and ready to go. Let's hope we're incident-free taking them over to the dinner."

Nerves twist my stomach. It's the event we've been working hard on, and it's finally here. I can't believe we're this close to pulling it off.

"You ready for this?" he asks, his gaze flitting over me.

"No. I'm sorta cursing Carl and Amanda right now. But ask me in three hours how I'm feeling and hopefully it will be a one-eighty."

"It's going to be amazing. We've dotted every *I* and crossed every *T*, Aria." He leans forward on the counter, his hands splayed against it, and I'm lost in the brilliant blue of his eyes.

I offer a brief smile, my only way of saying thanks right now. He can praise me all he wants in a few hours.

"We've done a good job so far," I tell him. "And you've done a lot of the tedious stuff. You drove all the way over to Colorado Springs to get the exact right sprigs of holly for the place settings."

"I don't question the methods behind your madness. I only wish you could have driven over with me."

Even as my chest burns at him wanting to be around me, I shrug, placing my hands near his on the counter and leaning even closer, willing my voice to stay neutral, casual. "Maybe we should drive to Colorado Springs another time, just for fun."

"There's a lot we could do for funsies. I think reading the obituaries with you would be fun."

"Wow." I tip my head back and peer at him through narrowed eyes.

"I meant that as a compliment." His gaze rakes over me. "You have a way of making random things exciting. And maybe the only reason

I'm dreading the dinner tonight is because that's one step closer to not being a co-host with you."

I feel my lips twitch. This is dangerous. But so good. So thrilling.

I nod, as if to say, me too, but take a half step back. "So, how's work been for you today."

He blows a little raspberry. "I have to represent someone I don't want to represent. I feel dirty just thinking about it."

"So, he's guilty, huh?"

"Yes." He nods. "It's hard to see his side, to have compassion. I don't exactly want to be the defense attorney in this scenario."

"Sounds like you're between a rock and a hard place," I say.

"One thing's for sure, at least I'm learning what types of law I don't want to practice. When I become partner and can have more of a say on what cases I do and don't take, I'll be happy to work on the more enjoyable things, like tax law, or property rights stuff."

"It all sounds unenjoyable." I make a cringey face.

"But I like it. You don't know enjoyable until you've read an eighty-page brief on a decades-long property line dispute."

I laugh. "I'll keep baking cheesecakes and trying to break into brand management, thank you very much."

There's a whoosh of air as the kitchen door opens. It's not Camilla, but Elijah, and I'm embarrassed that Theo and I were standing so close together. Maybe he didn't notice.

They say hi to each other and do a bro handshake sort of deal. The number one rule of nature is that guys can intrinsically do those little, complicated handshakes, no prep necessary.

"How did the deliveries go?" I ask him.

"Fine." He pauses as he takes off his coat, one I recognize as something Jesse used to wear. "Do you need me to take these cheesecakes to the event tonight for you?"

"No, I think we've got it covered, Elijah. Thanks." I glance around the room. "I think that's all we have for you today, unless Camilla says otherwise."

"She was counting batches of shortbread." Elijah hangs up his coat. "I am not going back in there until she's finished. She shushed me even before I said anything at all."

Theo and I laugh. "The counting is an intense job," I say.

"Why don't you have Elijah bring the cheesecakes over tonight?" Theo asks me. "That way we won't have to worry about them sliding around our cars."

"I'd love that, but I don't know if he wants to wait around. He wouldn't need to bring them for at least another hour or more."

"I'm good to wait. I can clean the bathroom or do whatever you need. I'm happy to stay." There's something in Elijah's eyes. Almost a pleading.

"Well, I mean, I guess that would be great." I flick a glance at Theo then turn back to Elijah. "Except, I'll pay you for driving the cheesecakes over. This isn't a Shorty's thing, it's a festival thing."

"Elijah was telling me he's been wanting more hours," Theo says.

"I've been meaning to bring it up again." He sways a little from side to side, his arms crossed over his chest. "I need all the money I can get. My mom recently got a second job, but she won't get a paycheck until the middle of December." He swallows hard and then, as if he said too much, he tries to backtrack. "But I was also thinking about getting one of those early morning jobs at the pasta factory, just to supplement this one." His smile is an attempt at brightness, but I can see through it. My heart plunges to my stomach.

"I didn't know that—" I stop myself. Elijah is eighteen. He doesn't want sympathy from me. "I've heard good things about working for the pasta plant. But yes, I'd love to give you all the hours we can. Sometimes it will be more, sometimes fewer."

"Yeah, yeah. I know. I don't mean to cause any issues."

"You're not," I insist. I give him a small slug on the shoulder. "Elijah Fleming, you can come to Camilla or me anytime, okay? Don't hesitate. You've been an amazing delivery professional. We gotta help each other out."

I smile and look at Theo, but he's looking past us, a million miles away. I have to clear my throat to get him to look at me.

He does and then turns to Elijah. "Would you be interested in custodial work at the firm?" Theo asks Elijah. "My boss needs someone new." The look Theo gives him is heavy, like he understands something neither of us do.

Elijah looks surprised. "Yeah, as long as it wouldn't interfere with this job." He glances over at me, and I offer a smile.

"I think it would only be for a couple of hours in the evenings, on weeknights," Theo says.

"But you're young, Elijah. You don't want to be working all the time. You gotta go have some fun."

Elijah's mouth tightens in a line.

"But you need fundage for the fun, right, Elijah?" Theo pats him on the shoulder. "I can send an application link to Aria, and she can forward it on to you. And I'll put in a good word with Weatherby."

He starts to back towards the door, and my first reaction is disappointment that I won't get to hang out with him until the event.

"Let's meet at Barrie Mansion at six-fifteen?" I ask him. "There are still a couple of place setting things I need to pick up from the party supply store."

He only nods once, looks at Elijah and then me again, and leaves.

It was amazing of Theo to be so helpful to Elijah. Still there was something there beneath the surface, something that I don't understand.

But I can't worry about that now. I have an event to co-host.

Chapter 21

Aria

I reach out to shake the hand of the mayor of Flinton, and then turn to his wife. "What are you hoping to find at the festival this year? Do you have anything specific in mind?"

She fingers a heavy-looking diamond necklace at her throat. "I can usually find the grandkids some fun things. They're still little enough that they're easy to please."

My mind shifts through the various vendors—the ones who haven't dropped out. "We have a couple of handcrafted toy maker booths. And then the toy store here in town is signed up again this year. Do you typically go for the current trends or more classic things?"

She shrugs. "It varies depending on what the grandkids are into. I'm thinking maybe those vintage-looking teddy bears. Will that vendor be there again this year?"

She must be referring to the quilter and dollmaker who drives over from Idaho.

"She will. And you can even reach out to her beforehand with any specific requests." I hand her my card. We all got a small box of them in our committee meeting. I like the feeling of pride and professionalism that wells up in me when I give her my card. It even has a photo of me wearing the Christmas blazer. "Just call or text me through that number there and I can send you her contact info."

I chat a little more with them and then move around the room. Theo's been standoffish. With the guests, he's his happy-go-lucky, friendly self. And I nearly had a heart attack when he showed up in his modern tan suit, close fitting and tailored to his body. He looked handsome in his Victorian clothing for the photo shoot. But if I know anything at all, I know that Theo Carter was born to wear this suit.

With me, though? Face to face, he seems off.

Maybe he's hungry like me. I venture back to the kitchen to see if the catering staff needs any help. The coordinator reassures me that they'll be plating in five minutes, so I hurry out to find Theo. We have to do the intro.

I can't see him, but the clock's ticking, so I step up on the platform in front and smooth the front of my turquoise silk dress with a sheer overlay. Tables covered in white tablecloths dot the room, and the string quartet is next to me, playing classical Christmas music. I grab the microphone and ask everyone in the room for their attention.

It's strange to hear my voice go through the PA system, but with the smiling, upturned faces of women in long evening dresses and men in black tie, I feel better. Calm.

We've worked hard for this. It's going to turn out.

The string quartet silences their music.

"Welcome, Ladies and Gentlemen, to the kickoff dinner for this year's Charles Dickens Christmas Festival here in New Hedge, Colorado!"

A cheer rises up through the room and before I know it, Theo's stepped to my side. His expression is still unreadable, so I continue on.

"We invite you to find a seat at one of the tables because we have a delicious meal for you, and I've been assured the wait staff will be bringing that out momentarily. I'm Aria Robinson, and on behalf of Theo Carter, my co-host, I wish to thank you for your support of this event. It's become one of the largest in the Northwestern United States, in large part, thanks to all of you and your undying support."

Another cheer goes up amongst the crowd. "Thank you for your passion for this cause," I continue. "It doesn't go unnoticed, especially this year when things have been tough after some disheartening news about the charity we formerly contributed to." I pause and then smile. "Rest assured, this year, the charitable donations collected at the festival will be going to Santa's Helpers, which we can verify will pass the majority of the funds earned directly to the kids in need."

I flash a look at Theo, unsure of how to continue. This was actually the part he had planned to say.

He reads my expression and takes the microphone from me.

"Thank you, Aria. As she said, I'm Theo Carter. And right now, I'd like to thank the committee. Prior to a few weeks ago, I had no idea the amount of work that goes into this. These people are dedicated to the cause and they're huge patriots of New Hedge and of the Intermountain West as a whole. Did you know that they meet at least once a week year-round?" He opens a hand out to his side. "You can identify them by their attractive Christmas-print blazers. They told me I couldn't wear mine, that I had to be a step above because I'm hosting. Which is a shame because boy, that blazer is my favorite article of clothing these days."

It's clear he's joking, and there's a polite smattering of laughter.

Yeah, I get you people. I have an unhealthy love for the blazers, I'll admit. But the getup he has going on tonight? Absolutely incredible.

Theo continues. "So, please thank them for all their hard work when you see them around here at the dinner, as well as at the festival, which I hope you're planning on attending daily. At least. If not more like three times a day."

He's good in front of a crowd.

Theo finishes up his portion of the intro, and everyone is seated by the time the first course of pear salad with balsamic and walnuts is brought out.

He's quiet as we sit at one of the tables in the front. I give my table decorations a cursory glance, satisfied with the ribbon-tied flatware, layers of patterned fabric napkins, and evergreen cuttings.

I press my glass to my lips and take a sip, both because I'm parched from all my running around and to give me something to do in the silence. We're sitting with a mix of committee members and industry elites from various corners of Colorado. There are a few different, quiet conversations going on with a backdrop of quartet music. Theo's not paying much attention to any of it.

Finally, I pipe up. "You're quiet tonight," I say to Theo. "Which is new." I laugh and instead of joining in like he usually does, his brow smashes down.

"I've got a lot on my mind. The firm, you know? Plus, I was thinking about how gorgeous you look in that dress," he says, his voice dark like gravel. He lifts his glass a smidge before taking a drink. But then he looks away, out over the crowd, unseeing.

"Thanks," I say quietly. I want to ask him what's wrong, but now is not the time or place.

I chat politely with the others. The rest of our table makes up for the quiet, which is good, because by the time the dessert course comes around, I'm fed up with his aloofness. We should be enjoying this impeccably delicious meal—the fruits of our labors. But he's distant. Which causes me to be even more hyperaware of everything he's doing.

And makes me wonder what he's upset about.

Just as the servers are bringing in the cheesecake with three small, pourable sauces on each plate—a rich chocolate ganache, a lemon and strawberry swirl, and a decadent pumpkin crème—Theo taps his butter knife on his glass.

"I wanted to let you know that Aria here actually baked these cheesecakes herself," he announces to the rest of the table. "And she made these sauces, too."

Our tablemates nod their approval and begin to eat. I don't want to stare at everyone while they're trying my dessert, so I instead turn to Theo and whisper, "Thanks."

He glances at me, for the first time since the salad course, but his smile doesn't reach his eyes. "I had to give credit where credit is due." He takes his fork, procures the tip of the slice and stows it to the side. Then, he scoops up another bite and dunks it in the chocolate ganache. He twists his mouth to one side in an attempt at a grin and then takes the bite.

I'm giddy as he closes his eyes while he chews. He's loving it, and I realize I love being the cause of his joy.

I really and truly care for him. I think I'm falling for him. Which is . . . not what I expected.

And might only be a byproduct of his distance tonight. Isn't that always what happens? We don't seem to care as much about the guy until he stops showering us with attention and then suddenly we're in love?

Which is messed up.

I *feel* messed up . . . discombobulated. And I've been feeling that way since finding out that Rob's getting married.

No, since Theo started coming around all the time.

But when seen through the lens of Theo coming around? I mean "messed up" in the best way possible.

I take a deep breath and let it out slowly, frustrated at all the places my mind can go in such a short amount of time. I have to be real with myself and admit that my feelings for Theo are strong, not because of his distance tonight. They're strong because of who he is, the person he is, and the way I feel when I'm around him.

My heart does a little skipping thing as Theo rotates his body towards me.

"That was a big sigh." His voice is chipper, but still, there's a mask over it, a careful covering. We have to talk about the kiss, about everything.

But not here.

"These shoes may be spectacular, but they pinch my toes," I say.

He glances down at my feet. "Slip 'em off. I won't tell anyone."

A light touch of desire pulses through me as I do it, without a second thought. It seems strange, but there's something a touch intimate about sliding off my shoes under our table and only he knows.

It doesn't make any sense. But since when have my feelings for Theo made sense?

I check myself.

They actually do. Of course they make sense. Theo is a good, good man. He's trustworthy and kind, funny, and thoughtful.

Of course my feelings make sense.

I have the strong urge to get up and take a walk, but my feet are relaxed without my shoes, and, as co-host, I can't very well traipse around barefoot, no matter how lovely that would feel.

"You did a good job with this. All of this," he says.

"You did, too," I tell him, my gaze dipping down to my half-eaten cheesecake.

"So, the next event is the ribbon-cutting ceremony?" he asks.

I nod. "And then we have to be at the festival as much as we can to mingle and take photos with everyone," I add.

Until Christmas Eve day, when the festival ends, and we go back to being just neighbors in downtown New Hedge.

He only nods, again deep in thought. He scoots his chair out and is about to stand, when he leans close to me and whispers, "Enjoy your toes' momentary freedom. Wish I could give them a solid rubdown for you." The heat of his breath is warming me from head to the very toes he wants to rub, and it nearly does me in.

Before I can even take a breath, he stands and leaves the table. I blink rapidly to try to get back into the moment, trying and failing to participate in the waning conversation as others are slowly leaving as well.

I only see him from a distance the rest of the night. Looks like he's trying to make a good effort to talk to as many of the dignitaries as he can. I'm so discombobulated that it's hard for me to comprehend how he can be calm, so perfectly put together at a time like this.

A time like this.

The moment I know, without a doubt, that I'm falling for Theo Carter.

Chapter 22

Theo

I walk back and forth in front of the bakeshop entrance like a sucker, freezing my booty off, the night air biting at my face and hands. There's so much I want to tell Aria, so much I'd like to explain and do.

Besides, I owe her a foot rub.

"Owe" her is a stretch. I only expressed my desire to do that, never promised I would. But this woman is in my blood, and when I began to drive home after the dinner, my car took me here instead, without my permission.

So now I'm sitting in my car, staring up at the dark window above the bakeshop. I don't know why I'm here, but I do know it's probably not a good idea.

I get a text from Weatherby, which says for me to call him as soon as I can. I move to place the call and then stop. I bargain with myself. I'll reach out to Aria, see if she's okay with me coming up for a little while, and then, because I know I need to call my boss, that will be my motivation to leave.

There. If I do that, I won't stay too long.

What am I even doing here? I freak out a little, thinking about earlier, when pieces of the puzzle finally clicked, when I realized exactly who that Elijah-kid is.

A chill goes over me again. And the drive I feel to help him is strong. He doesn't deserve the life he's been forced to live. Nothing about his situation is okay.

I mostly kept my distance from Aria tonight and that won't do. I regret it. I think I was still feeling thrown by my discoveries concerning Elijah, mourning alongside him—in my own way.

I have to see Aria again. Tonight.

I pace some more, and then make up my mind, using my key to open the door to the firm. If she doesn't want to see me right now, it's fine. It's nearly ten o'clock.

I take the stairs two at a time, enter my office, inhale, exhale, and knock on the wall.

"Aria?"

There's no sound through the wall and after waiting, I try again.

Still nothing, so I busy myself with answering a few work emails, all the while, my ear trained on next door.

Finally, a rustling sound comes from her apartment, followed by footfalls. I go back to the wall and knock again.

"Milady? How are those poor little toes?"

I might imagine it, but I think I hear a low chuckle from her as the bed springs squeak. "Like they've been singed with the devil's scepter," she says.

I laugh and shake my head. "Want that foot rub?"

"Does an owl hoot? Do pigs snort? Does a kitten meow?"

"Well then. It's imperative that I come and remedy the situation," I say. "I'll slay the devil and break his scepter in two." I feel dumb, with my all-over-the-place British accent.

"You'd better. I'll come unlock the bakeshop door."

I don't know why I'm doing this, playing this dangerous game. And it's only dangerous not because Aria is . . . whatever. It's dangerous because I'm so gone for her, and I'm not sure how she feels about me.

And I can't forget about returning Weatherby's call. Reminding myself of Weatherby might be a handy thing if I start getting too caught up in Aria.

I hurry back downstairs out the door, and to the bakeshop. When she opens the door, I see she's in sweats and a T-shirt. "Hey," she says, the shadow of a not-quite-there smile on her lips.

"How are you?"

"I was getting ready to wash my face."

"Glad you got a chance to get into some comfortable clothes. I'm still in this." I open up one side of the unbuttoned suit coat.

"You look nice in that suit."

"Well, thanks." Usually, in the past, when a woman would give me a compliment, I'd soak it all in, use it to bolster my strength, and then boast some more or fish for compliments.

But with Aria, it's different. I'm not going to use anything she says to me as a cheap façade to puff myself up.

"Come in," she says. "I'll show you my new wall hangings."

I follow her as she walks through the bakeshop front of house, the kitchen, and down the hall to the staircase in the back.

"Wall hangings? I barely have anything up at my place and I've lived there ever since I graduated from law school, over three years."

"I've been at my parents' house for so long that I was excited for a place I could do my own thing with."

After she points out a series of square landscape and still-life canvases edged in liquid gold, we settle in beneath them on her sofa. "Tell me about your parents," I say.

She shrugs, picking off a piece of lint from her sweatpants. "I won't sugar coat it. Individually, they're great. But they might be the most unhappy happily-married couple I know."

"Oh, no."

"I get the impression they'd like to make an Olympic sport out of complaining to one another about all the stuff that annoys them." She smiles broadly, but it doesn't reach her eyes. "And my grandparents divorced a long time ago. My dad's parents were only together long enough to have my dad and then they split up. I think the universe is trying to tell me something."

"What's that?"

"To not fall in love." She laughs, but there's pain behind her eyes.

"But were you in love? With Rob?"

Her gaze darts to her lap, her bottom jaw moving back and forth. "This again?" She gives a hollow laugh. "I think Rob was an unwitting shield to protect me from falling in love. Sadly."

"How so?"

She waves me away. "Can we talk about something else right now? Our plan to save the festival?"

I nod. "You start. I'll take care of your feet."

"You want to give me a foot rub for real?"

When I nod, she sits up and rotates to pound the throw pillows with her fist a couple of times. She gets comfortable, relaxing against the pillows, and I have a hard time not staring at her. She's like a princess on a chaise lounge.

"Are you sure you want to do this? I have ballerina feet." She makes a face.

I grab a pillow that's fallen to the floor and use it to prop her feet up. "I like your feet," I insist.

They're tanned, with a defined and high instep. Her ankles are strong. Her toenails sport dark pink polish. I pick one foot up and settle it in my lap, resting the other foot on the pillow.

"I have corns and calluses. I even had stress fractures from my pointe shoes."

"Well, then you have even more reason for some TLC."

She gives a soft, low moan as I knead circles into the arches of her foot.

If we don't start talking about the festival, I'm going to be too distracted to think straight at all.

"I have to admit, I've never paid much attention to the festival," I say. "How's it going to be on opening day?"

Her eyes pop open wide—brown pools of excitement. "If we get an opening day, it's the best kind of madhouse you've ever seen."

"We're going to get our opening day. And it's going to be a success. I can feel it."

"I hope so," she says, letting her eyes sink closed.

"So, we're supposed to show up, say our spiel, and move out of the way?" I ask.

"Basically," she concedes, her eyes still closed. "The media will be there for the ribbon cutting, so I think we should practice how we might answer questions. Do you think the news stations will be big jerks and mention Carl and Amanda?"

"I don't know, but we need to be prepared either way."

"What do we even say?"

I study the paintings above our heads. "Do our best to answer in one vague sentence and then change the subject."

She nods. "Here's a change of subject for you." She opens her eyes and straightens. "Theo? Was there something wrong earlier? You seemed kind of down."

I shift in the sofa, my back feeling tired. "It's my pro bono case." It does have to do with the case. She just doesn't yet know in what way. I can't tell her because of client confidentiality.

"When's the court date?"

"Next week."

"Have you figured out your approach with the judge?"

"I think so."

I've spoken briefly with the prosecuting attorney and he's willing to consider some good options. It's just that lately, whenever I'm working on the case, I freeze, lost in thoughts of my father.

There's so much about this I can't talk with Aria about. "But let's practice some talking points for the media."

And so we do. Me obsessing over her calves and feet, and the feel of her skin on my fingertips, while she adds notes to a doc on her phone.

Far too soon, she drags her feet towards her and wraps her arms around her knees. "Thank you for that. I think I'll be able to walk tomorrow without dying."

"I'm happy to help. I like taking care of you, Aria."

She stares at me, her gaze moving, rapid fire, from one eye to the other. "I'd better call it a night." She stands and stretches her arms over her head, the hem of her shirt riding up just enough for me to see a flash of skin right above her waistband before she lowers her arms.

Okay. I need to get out of here. My feelings are like clean socks in the dryer, slamming against the drum—mixed up, falsely secure, heated.

"Thanks for coming by," she says. "I feel better about things now that we've had a chance to plan."

"Me, too." Without thinking, I wrap an arm around her waist, stepping closer to her. Her bottom lip drops open in surprise and then she smiles just enough to give me permission.

I close my mouth against hers. I'm cautious and taking it a lot slower than my instinct.

This is Aria. It's important to get this right.

I cradle her head as she returns the kiss, and now we're really kissing, her hands going from my chest around to my back so she can press me closer. I widen my stance so I don't stumble. The way she's teasing my mouth with hers brings a mystical air, where the only sound I hear is the beating of her heart, the pulse in her neck against my wrists. And when she sighs and parts her lips, I have to force myself to step back.

We say nothing. But I feel the beginnings of a smile dance along my lips when I see the same on hers.

I've thought of this moment, of kissing Aria for real, for two years.

Chapter 23

Aria

Theo's mouth on me last night? Fodder for every single thought I've had ever since.

I fell asleep thinking of how it felt, how sliding my palms along his strong, lithe shoulders and around to the back of his neck sent cascades of goosebumps throughout my arms and legs. I woke up thinking of the soft pressure of his lips on mine, how blissfully breathless he made me.

I thought our first kiss was good—too good—and the forbidden nature of it made it even more thrilling.

Now? Nothing could have prepared me for how his kisses make me feel.

Our second kiss sent the first one to a vague sense of fluffy giddiness in my mind. I'm undone by last night, enthralled by the knowledge that all my time with Rob was like wandering in a desert, a very stale desert.

Theo is my manna, and now that I know what it's like to kiss him, I can't go back to the manna-free life, back to a hunger I didn't even understand that I had.

I'm blaming this state of mind for the way I whimsically—irresponsibly?—

pressed that "apply now" button a few times this morning, filling things out and attaching my resume and portfolio with the kind of reckless abandon that can only be attributed to the post-kiss hangover.

It's fine. I probably won't even get an interview.

Camilla is frustratingly perfect at reading my aura or mood or whatever, so of course, she knows right when she sees me what has happened.

"I'm happy for you," she says, with actual tears pooling in her eyes. "You two could get married on my anniversary! That would make it so special." Her words tumble out of her, so rapid I can't get a word in edgewise. "And we could plan to get pregnant at the same time, and then I'll have a boy and you'll have a girl and they'll be best buddy cousins and—"

"Camilla!" My growl is sharp. "You always do this."

"Do what?"

"Jump to the most impossible conclusions. Besides. We kissed before, remember? It's not a big deal."

Lies.

It's a very big deal.

"I know. But that was a rebound, crazy psycho kiss." She flings her arms around. She's the most dramatic of all hand talkers. "Now, your nervous system has calmed down, everything's good. You're both clear-minded." She claps her hands. "Which makes me so happy."

Before she can start crying again, I tighten my apron with a forceful yank.

"Look, it's all very new." I'm whispering, but I step towards her, milking my height to intimidate her. And I don't feel the least bit sorry about it. "I need you to not say anything to anyone. Especially your husband."

She puffs out a breath. "I—" She clamps her mouth shut and breathes heavily out of her nose. "Okay. I can respect that. But you don't understand how hard this is for me. And Jesse wouldn't say anything to Theo."

I roll my eyes. "Yeah right. He might not mean to, but he will. Or Theo will sense he knows or—"

"Why can't people know? I mean, not the general public, but why can't a few select people know?"

"Know what?" Elijah breezes through the doors.

"Well, didn't *you* pick a fine time to get here early?" I say, throwing my hands up in disgust. And then I regret it, because his face instantly falls.

"Elijah asked for more hours and I said, especially during the holidays, that would be awesome. We can use the extra help." Camilla places a hand on his elbow and steers him so that her five-foot-two frame is between us.

"I'm glad you'll be here more," I tell him. "I'm sorry for what I said just now. You know we think you're the best, right Elijah?"

He only gives a wan smile, not meeting my gaze. I make a rash decision to go out on a limb. "And if you ever need anything else, like a listening ear or whatever, we're here for you, okay? Camilla and I." I toss a glance in her direction. "We remember how things were after graduating high school. So many expectations, so many people asking questions about future plans . . ."

I trail off because the look on his face is one of pure embarrassment mixed with *Lady, you don't know anything about my life.*

"Agreed." Camilla whips her head around to look at Elijah behind her and then back at me. She doesn't have her hairnet on yet because she hasn't started baking for the day, so her blonde curls are free to fly around her face at will with every movement. I'm always in awe of her hair.

"So, let's do our opening dance and get on with this day. The festival is almost here." Camilla leads us in the dance we used to do in high school at the football games and have done ever since she took over Shorty's.

"S-H, S-H-O, S-H-O-R-T-Y-S! Shorty's!" *Clap, clap,* "Shorty's!" *Clap, clap.*

Elijah goes through the movements, but there's definitely something off about him. I probably needed to pay more attention in my child development class in college, then maybe I could know how to approach him, how to let him know we care.

But for now, I can only show up for him the best way that I can without coming on too strong.

I spend the morning baking cheesecakes, allowing my mind to repeatedly circle back around to Theo and every amazing little and big thing he does. When that isn't happening—which is hardly ever—I tune into Merre telling us funny stories about her college days when she was a dorm mom.

I get bold around lunchtime and text Theo, letting him know I'm thinking of him and that I'd love to make him a sandwich with one of Danene's croissants if he's hungry.

His text is a little lackluster. *Ditto. And I wish I could have lunch with you, but I have back-to-back clients for the next few hours. We'll be in touch.*

Not a bad response. It's fine.

But that's the problem. It's fine. Bland. Generic. Our kiss last night wasn't bland or generic . . . nothing about the man has ever been bland or generic.

During my lunch break, I go upstairs to my place to search the online job websites. I want to work for a PR firm, I want new challenges, new clients. I need my own thing—my own path.

When Theo comes into the bakeshop right before closing, my heart does a *mayday, mayday* sort of thing. Because Theo is definitely not okay. To the naked eye of a random person, sure, he probably seems great.

But I've spent the last several weeks studying him on a higher level. I've done a deep dive into Theo-dom, and my research tells me something is definitely off.

"How are things?" Theo asks, his voice chirps like a parrot—a falsehood.

"Great. But I can tell you're not great," I say.

And *I'm* not great, but I won't get into that right now with Camilla, Merre, and Elijah in the kitchen.

"It's the pro bono case. But due to client confidentiality, I can't say anything about that..." he trails off and then whips his head around and points to one of our little bistro tables. "When you're finished with work, maybe we can talk?" His eyes have dark smudges under them, like maybe he didn't sleep well last night.

I nod and punch a few more figures into the app on the bakeshop iPad, the one we have to update every day at closing. But my heartbeat stuffs up my ears, and a sick sense of dread comes over me.

I finish clearing the till and then go to join Theo just as Camilla, Merre, and Elijah walk through the swinging door, mid-laughter, finished with work for the day. It's as if Theo is standing on the edge of a storm cloud, just from their presence in the room.

What is going on?

That's when I hear Elijah clear his throat and walk to our table. Camilla and Merre are in quiet conversation back at the counter as he approaches us, his head down, one hand pressing against the back of his neck. He raises his gaze when he reaches us.

"You're my dad's lawyer, aren't you?"

Chapter 24

Aria

Theo's expression hardens like a drying clay face mask. He seems lost in thought before he comes to himself.

"If your dad is Marty Fleming, then yes, I am." Theo slowly rises to his feet, his tie moving slightly as it hangs from his neck. His face holds both anxiety and dread.

Camilla and Merre hesitate by the kitchen door. Camilla says, "Whoa—"

My sentiments exactly. Theo is my coworker's father's defense attorney?

Elijah holds up his hands. "My mom mentioned your name last night, and I figured out it was you. Just letting you know who I am."

Theo nods, flexing his jaw. He stares at the tabletop. "I had no idea until a couple of days ago." He looks up at Elijah. "I figured you were probably Marty's son and looking over the notes confirmed that."

Elijah only swallows and shifts in his stance.

"Small world." Theo chuffs a colorless laugh. He sits back down, but his back and shoulders are rigid. "I want you to know I'm sorry about all that's happened with your dad."

Elijah tosses a glance at Camilla and then at me. "I should have told you that my dad stole from his employer. He took money from his boss's safe and then got caught trying to return it." Elijah says, his voice barely above a whisper.

Merre pushes open the kitchen door. "I need to get going, so . . ."

"Thanks, Merre. We'll see you tomorrow." Camilla clutches Merre's arm briefly before joining us at the table.

I turn to Theo, feeling my brows knit together. "I'm really sorry your family's having to go through this." I gesture to a chair. "Have a seat. Why didn't you tell us about your dad?"

Elijah swallows hard and puts his hands low on his hips, his head sinking low. He doesn't sit. "Because it's embarrassing." His head rears back, his voice full of venom. "And I didn't want to be judged for my dad's stupidity."

The color has drained from Elijah's face. He turns to Camilla. "I should have told you before. I understand if you don't trust me. He stole from his employer, so if you need to find someone else to do the deliveries . . ."

"Elijah," Camilla guides him at the elbow to sit down next to me. "You and your dad are two separate people. Let's talk about this, okay? We need you to stay at Shorty's. Please? Don't get any ideas about quitting now that we know a bit about what's going on."

She sweeps her gaze over him. "I trust you not to steal. I know you wouldn't do that."

Elijah hesitates and then lets out a breath. "Okay."

I hazard a glance at Theo and his scowl has reached new heights. I didn't know Theo was capable of scowling so hard. "You guys talk it out. I better go." He stands from the table, fussing with his laptop bag. "And look, Elijah. I've had some personal issues I've been dealing with." He pauses, pinching the skin between his eyebrows. "I haven't been the best defense attorney for your dad yet. But I will be. We're going to turn this thing around, okay?"

"Theo," I say, rising from my chair, my heart thudding against my rib cage. "Can we meet up later? Maybe get a bite to eat?"

"Yeah. Sure. I'll be in touch." And he leaves, a cloud of heaviness trailing behind him.

"Elijah," Camilla says, slumping into the chair Theo was just sitting on. "You are under no obligation to tell us anything about what happened with your dad. But we'd love to know how you're doing with all this. And your family. Your mom. I'm sure it's been hard."

"If you want to," I add. "If you'd rather not, that's fine."

He runs a hand across his ear before shaking his head, his gaze trained on the tabletop. "I really don't—" He sighs. "My dad isn't like this, okay? He's not some deadbeat, always in and out of jail. He's never stolen anything before. My parents didn't have much money, and my mom was looking for another job. They were separated when he did it. I don't think he was himself." His fists ball tightly on the table. "I didn't think my dad could ever do something like that."

"I'm sure it was a shock," I offer. I know, legally, I can't ask him any questions, nor would I. But I care a lot about this kid, and I'm inflamed by how much this has hurt Elijah and his family.

"Believe me, he wasn't like this," Elijah says. "I don't know what got into him. When he left the house, he was really depressed. He moved to some old apartment on the other side of town. And when my mom reached out to ask him for money, he said he didn't have any. I think he took it from the employer as a last resort." He gives Camilla and me a pointed look. "Not that that makes it right."

"No, it doesn't," Camilla offers. "But it sounds like he was going through some rough stuff and maybe he felt it *was* his last resort."

"My mom said he took it, kept it in his car for a couple of days, and then went to put it back, which is when he got caught. He didn't spend any of it. Still counts as theft, though. And of course, putting it back looks a whole lot like taking it out. His boss called the police, and he was incarcerated for a couple of weeks."

"Do you know when the hearing is?"

"Next week. I don't care about Christmas gifts and stuff, but my little sisters do. And my mom started working at a doctor's office, but she won't get her first paycheck until the middle of December and every penny of that's going to all these bills from the last few months." He sighs and puts his head down, massaging his closed eyes with his thumbs. "This is why I wanted to work more hours, and why I wanted to get a second job."

"It's all really heavy. It would be a lot for anyone to deal with," I say.

Camilla nods. "We're here for you, Elijah. Let us know if there's something we can help with, okay?"

"Thanks." Elijah's voice is gruff. "I should go home. My mom's working for the after-hours clinic tonight, so I need to feed my sisters and make sure they go to bed on time."

"Your mom's fortunate to have you," I say.

"Yeah, well, I might be the man of the house now, especially if dad goes to prison. They'll probably get divorced."

There's nothing to say to that. We sit there, the silence engulfing us, until Camilla straightens. "I can give you your paycheck early. I'd be happy to do that if it would help?"

"No." He gives a quick shake of his head. "But thank you." He stands, mumbles "I'll see you in the morning" under his breath, and leaves.

After he's gone, Camilla lets out a long, slow breath. "I can't believe it. This is awful."

"There's got to be something we can do. Maybe an anonymous donation? Maybe we could do a fundraiser for the family to help them get through the holidays."

"Yes. That's a great idea," she says.

"Except, Camilla? You have zero time. Like none." I pat her shoulder. "How about this? How about we try to add them to Santa's Helpers. That way part of the donations at the festival could go to them."

"Can you do that?" Camilla's expression is doubtful. "The festival is starting. And Elijah's dad's case has been in the news. I don't know how understanding the community will be, you know? Would people be concerned about helping a family whose father is accused of theft?"

"I don't care," I say, my voice getting louder. "Elijah, his mom, and sisters did nothing wrong. I don't think we need to mention it at all. They're a family in need. That's it." Possibilities start forming in my head. "We can do this. I don't think it's too late to add them."

I stand, my mind a jumble of ideas. I have to help the Flemings. And I'm going to start by talking with Theo.

Chapter 25

♥

Theo

New Hedge isn't famous only for its Charles Dickens Christmas Festival, we have other cool things here, too. Like a world-renowned duck pin bowling team—a team of eight sixty-somethings who won the championship in Sioux City, Iowa last year. And the Lucky Cosmos, a mom-and-pop burger joint where the vinyl booths are made to look like flying saucers and the servers are dressed up like aliens.

It's epic. And the fact that Aria wanted to eat here makes her that much cooler.

"I've got to admit, I wasn't sure you'd go for the Lucky Cosmos idea." Aria slides into the booth and does that shifting, sliding, moving thing. Is it ever not awkward to try to get from point A to point B in a restaurant booth?

"Are you kidding? The burgers here melt in your mouth."

"I'm a slave to the fries, personally." She brightens in a smile, but then the corners of her eyes pinch together. "Theo, it's crazy you're Elijah's dad's attorney."

A burn moves across my chest. "Yeah."

"Elijah's great. It's unfortunate that the family is in this position."

I pinch my inner cheek in between my teeth. I have to control myself. There's something about criminals that makes me petty. "Elijah is an awesome kid."

"He is. He's always on time, or early, for his shifts. He goes above and beyond to get things done. He's even good at cleaning bathrooms. His momma taught him a thing or two."

We order our burgers and fries, but somehow have the good sense to order water cups instead of the soda or milkshakes that look so good.

Aria's wearing a thin, burnt-orange sweater and jeans with holes in all the right places, so I can see her strong thighs. Her hair is in a loose braid that hangs over one shoulder. I can hardly stand how beautiful this woman is.

We're discussing her marketing program when a waiter wearing a green and silver alien costume brings out our food.

"Your burger good?" Aria asks around bites, bringing up a napkin to dab at the corner of her mouth. I try not to be distracted by her lips.

I nod since I'm still trying to chew. Once I swallow, I respond. "No news is good news on the festival, I guess. Seems like it's happening. You ready for it to open?"

"I'm excited. But I'm not ready to give up my co-host title on Christmas Eve."

"The Christmas blazer. Are they going to have to pry it out of your cold, dead hands?"

She laughs, shrugs, and chews her bottom lip. "Maybe. I was thinking, if they wanted us to, we could come back next year? And that way, the blazer can stay in my closet, where it belongs."

To allow myself to think of next year cracks open a rock in my chest. And what about all the time in between? I'd go to meetings with her every week. Plus, I'd be working next to where she works and lives? It sounds good. Very good.

"I can't believe I'm about to say this, but yeah. I could do next year."

"You can't believe you'd want to be my co-host again?" Aria asks in mock dismay. "It about killed you, didn't it?"

I swirl a fry in smoky ketchup. "Yes. And I'd only agree to co-host again so I can wear the breeches."

She tilts her head back in a laugh then grows serious. "You liked doing this with me. I know you did."

"I did. I do." My gaze darts down to her mouth, but I quickly go back to looking her in the eye. She has to understand that I'm completely gone for her, and it's about a lot more than the kissing.

She breaks my gaze. "So, I was thinking about talking to the committee and Santa's Helpers about adding the Fleming family to the charity recipient list."

"Wasn't that list finalized weeks ago?"

"Yeah, but they're in dire need. Elijah doesn't deserve this."

I don't say anything for a while, fighting with myself about how to respond. "I see parts of myself in Elijah. I'd love to help the family somehow. I can't do that until the judge has heard the case." I massage my temples and groan. "I don't like practicing criminal law."

"Hopefully you can keep Marty out of prison and they can rebuild, you know? Work on healing their marriage. If he goes to prison for this?" Aria frowns. "You can't let that happen to this poor family."

"I can't let that happen? Unfortunately, I'm not the judge."

"Right. But you have a lot of influence." She sets her burger back down without taking her next bite.

"I don't have much experience with this. Weatherby's helping me along, but this is out of my comfort zone. I'll do my best, but getting him out of serving a prison sentence? Is that really the best thing for him?"

"He didn't spend any of the money, Theo." She's stirring her ice water with her straw, staring at it. "Not a penny of it. He was putting it back. He's already served jailtime." She stares at me. "Why should he go to prison?"

I shift in the booth and rest my arm along the back rest. "I don't make the laws, Aria. He stole money. A lot of money. Just because he suddenly grew a conscience doesn't mean there shouldn't be some consequences for his actions."

"So you're not going to ask the judge for leniency, even after all the evidence points to a man who deserves it?" She moves the water cup off to the side, one less thing in between us. "Has he ever stolen anything before, Theo?"

I discharge a grunted breath. "Marty's maybe never gotten caught for stealing prior to this, but he has a criminal record. Possession, Aria. It was a long time ago, but the judge is going to take one look at that and make up his mind right then and there."

She pulls tightly on her thick paper napkin, smoothing it on the table with force. "Sounds like you're the one who's done that. Made up your mind." She balls up the napkin. "You're a generous guy. A nice guy. You have a chance to make a difference in this family's lives, but you're not going to try?"

"What's of most benefit to them in the long run? I can offer the judge a plea deal. Then Marty serves time for his crime, gets off on probation, and justice is served, then the family can be reunited. If the judge decides to let him off scot-free? Well, then great. But I'm not going to make that decision for him."

"This feels personal, Theo." She leans forward and digs her pointer finger against the tabletop. "I don't understand why."

I stare at my food, not wanting it anymore. "I don't tolerate fathers who abandon their families. It's an epidemic, Aria. And I'm not going to advocate that this father get a slap on the wrist for bailing when things got hard."

Her eyes soften in confusion. "This isn't about bailing when things got hard." Now her voice is louder. "This is a criminal case. It's not your place to be thinking of him in that context." She swallows hard, her eyes wide. "Maybe you should tell Weatherby to assign someone else to it."

That's what I would prefer but it's too late for that. Besides, I have to do whatever Weatherby asks of me. "I don't want to advocate for Marty." At the sound of her protest, I continue. "I know I have to. It's my job. And seeing how this has affected Elijah makes me sad."

She blinks rapidly, staring at her Styrofoam plate.

"I think your judgment has been clouded by your past experiences," she says. "What your dad did, abandoning your family, was completely unacceptable, and I'm so sorry he did that and that you've had to spend your life trying to heal from that."

I feel my chin rise without my permission. "It sucked big time. But I got over it a long time ago."

Aria doesn't look convinced.

My shoulders slump, fatigue overtaking me. "I don't understand why I'm being villainized for trying to uphold the law here."

"It's Elijah, and he's my friend. And it's Christmas."

"Christmas? Does that make a difference?" I choke out a laugh. "Hey, I have an idea. Let's let a criminal go free as a Christmas present." I dig the knuckle of my thumb in my forehead. "It doesn't work like that."

"He's not a hardened criminal. Showing some compassion and mercy could go a long way. If he gets put in the system and his wife leaves him for good? I don't know, Theo. There's a lot at play here."

"Exactly. There's a lot at play. That's what I'm trying to tell you. I don't want to hurt the family." I open my arms wide. She wants the truth? I'll tell her the truth.

"That was me. I *was* that family. I *was* Elijah. All I'm saying is no one was there to prosecute my father when he didn't pay a dollar of child support. When he ruined my mom's and his own reputations, which blacklisted her from all the big circles, which gave her all these mental and emotional blocks so she didn't want to practice law anymore." I take a breath, but it does nothing to calm me.

"She didn't have it in her to practice and had to quit," I say, and I watch as Aria's face falls more and more with every confession I'm making. "He took the family money and ran. He should have been put in jail for what he did, but no one cared enough to prosecute. My mom just wanted him to stay away from us." I give a humorless laugh. "He certainly did that."

Aria is breathing heavily. "I'm so sorry your own father did that to you. But Marty Fleming isn't your father!"

I rear back as if I've been slapped. "I've never said he was," I say quietly. "All I'm saying is I won't be part of this problem, this system that doesn't hold people accountable for their actions. Charges are dropped all the time. You have meth babies detoxing in hospitals and where are their fathers? Off repeating their mistakes over and over again." My voice cracks. "Fatherlessness is an epidemic."

"This case is about the theft, not if he abandoned his family or not." Her voice is quieter now, and I look away when I see the concern in her eyes. "You're going after him for something you have no business going after."

She shakes her head and gets up from the table, her food grown cold. She stands at the edge, turns away, then turns back to the fries. After staring at them a moment, she grabs two, bites them in half, chews, and swallows.

"This isn't about Marty or Elijah," she says. "This is about *you*, Theo. The best way to help Elijah and his mom and sisters is to figure out yourself." She takes a step from the table.

"Where are you going?"

"I need a second." She flicks me a glance, her fawn eyes soft. Tortured. "I'll be in the bathroom."

"Wait." I get up from the table and take a few steps to fall into step beside her. I grasp her wrist, gently. "There's something else. Weatherby reached out last night, and I called him after I left your place. He got an anonymous phone call, obviously from someone who is so bored with their life they have nothing better to do than peek in windows and make judgements. But, look. Remember when we kissed? The first time?" I let go of her wrist.

She nods and then screws up her features, opening her eyes just enough to see me, her head cocked back. "At the firm?"

"Yeah. Well, apparently someone was walking by. I'm guessing to visit their storage unit. That's all I can figure. But they saw the kiss and eventually called Weatherby. Told him they thought he had a right to know."

Aria's gone pale, and she's chewing on her bottom lip.

When she doesn't say anything, I do. "It's okay. There was nothing wrong with a goodbye kiss. Nothing wrong at all . . ."

I wait until she meets my gaze, and the look I'm giving is, I hope, letting her know just how *not* wrong it was.

Her tongue darts out and she licks her lips. "So, are we in trouble or something?"

I smile. "No. Weatherby had to tell me about it, but he's not concerned. Frankly, I think he was sorta happy for me. He told me a few months ago I needed a private life, that I'd been working too much."

She steps to me, clasping both of my hands in hers. "There's nothing we can do about it now. It's out there. People know."

"The community has been talking about this, you and me, ever since the billboards of us went up."

"I know. Let's let it ride. Let's see what happens."

She brushes her lips against my cheek.

I have a lot to work on. Aria is probably right. I need to figure out a plan of what to do. All I know is, I want to be a better man.

And for the first time, I might have a plan that will help me do that.

Chapter 26

Aria

One of the festival committee head honchos, Marjorie, leans back in her office chair, a small smile crossing her lips. Her office is wall-papered in blue and green paisley on the top half and plaid on the bottom half. Odd, but somehow, it works. She's got one of those plug-in air fresheners, and the strong scent of Christmas evergreen is stinging my nose.

"So, is it too late to add them?" I ask, apprehension making my lungs tight.

"Santa's Helpers got back to me. They said if we can raise enough funds to surpass our goals, the excess can go to the Fleming family." She pauses. There's something hanging in the air.

"That's great," I say. "They have an eighteen-year-old son. A twelve-year-old daughter. And six-year-old twin girls. And can it be anonymous? I really don't want them to suspect that the festival or I had anything to do with it."

"Of course." She hesitates. "Aria, I'll be honest with you. I don't know if there will be extra for that family. I'm starting to wonder if there will be enough for the originals that Santa's Helpers designated weeks ago. With sponsorships and ticket sales down, the number of booths involved at an all-time low, and, in some circles, a negative attitude towards the festival, I would be shocked if we met our charitable goals this year."

I rotate my silver and turquoise ring around my finger. I got it from the festival the year I graduated from college. "At least it's still happening. I feel like if it's still going on, and we all show up ready to go, people are going to come."

She smiles sadly. "This has been a year, hasn't it?" She shakes her head. "I'm starting to wonder if it's time for me to hang up my blazer. It's been rough."

"What can I do?"

"You and Theo have been wonderful. There's still a lot of excitement around you two. And if the rumors are to be believed, it's not a front for the sake of the festival." Her grin broadens.

"That's something I'm still not quite sure about." I will my smile to recede, but it's not obeying me right now. "Regardless, if all the data points are lower than ever, what good have our efforts done?"

The dam in my chest that has plagued me since the news of Carl and Amanda shifts ever so slightly. Because now I'm a tiger, prowling for her prey.

Maybe that's too violent.

I don't feel violent. I feel ready. Ready for this one last push to save the festival—the only happy Christmas memory from my childhood that I have.

Things are uncharacteristically slow at the bakeshop, so I'm working on one of the festival's rebranding projects on one of the tables out front. Marjorie's comments yesterday are lodged in my consciousness, and I can't seem to shake the dread. Dread for seeing what actually happens on opening day and for the rest of the festival. Worry over what I'll do if no one comes, no one buys anything, and no one puts cash in the big plastic stocking.

I swallow down the last of my tea, the bitter dregs perfect for my foul mood. There's a steel trap over my insides, protecting them from harm.

My phone rings and it's a number I don't recognize.

"I'm calling on behalf of Wolfe Strategies, a PR and brand management firm in Highlands Ranch." The woman on the other end introduces herself. "Wolfe is hiring a new specialist. We received your application and are wondering if you'd like to come in for an interview?"

"Really? I've been thinking of looking for a new position." My heartbeat increases in speed, zooming through me as I wonder if this is real.

I think it is real. I'm Aria Freaking Robinson! Hear me roar! Or whatever sound a "wolf" makes.

Hear me growl?

I shake my head. I can't be monologuing to myself right now. "Yes, I can come in for an interview, for sure."

The woman explains more details about the job, and with every word, I want it more and more. "One of our specialists was pregnant and planning to quit the job after the baby came, but she gave birth prematurely. We're scrambling to find her replacement. Is there any way you could come in tomorrow for an interview?" she asks. "Morning would be best for us."

"Well, I'm technically still at my other job, but I could quit that after Christmas. If I can come to an interview at nine, I can arrange it with my job. My employer is super flexible."

"Great. See you at nine tomorrow."

My heart rises a little from my melancholy over the festival. With any luck, I could get this job and do what I love—finally. I want to call Theo and tell him the good news, but I hear the kitchen door swing open.

Oh, no. I'm not ready for this moment of reckoning, of actually taking the plunge and going for it.

"Camilla." I stand as she comes in. "Did you overhear my conversation?"

You know that heart thing? The one that softened a little when Wolfe Strategies called? Well, now the steel trap is back, clenching it tight.

She blinks and then nods, her chest heaving. I can't read her expression.

"Was that Wolfe Strategies?" she asks, a smile playing about her lips.

I rush to her. "Y-yeah. How did you know?"

She smiles, but her eyes are pooling with tears. "Their HR rep called me yesterday since you listed me as an employer."

I nod. "They're based in Highlands Ranch, but I could work remotely from home three days a week, so that's nice. And I told them I couldn't officially start until the Christmas rush here is over."

Camilla nods once. "That was always the plan, right? You help me get this off the ground, you get your marketing degree, and then you go get your swanky brand management job." She grabs the ends of her apron strings and pulls tight. "I've been encouraging you to do this, but now that it might actually happen, I ..."

My throat is thick. "It might not even happen, Camilla. I'm not sure I want it to. I'll go to the interview, but chances are, it won't pan out."

"It's going to pan out. If not with Wolfe, then with somewhere else. You set aside your own life three years ago because I was drowning after Grandpa died." She pulls at the hair at the crown of her head. "*Drowning*. Remember that? And you helped me. You believed in me." Tears spring up in Camilla's eyes. "But you doing my marketing and running the register for the rest of your life? That's not what you want. You want corporate. You need a job where you can wear all the blazers you want to."

I laugh as I wipe my eyes with the back of my hand. "Now you're talking. And listen, you can't get rid of me completely. As long as I'm in the area, I'll make the cheesecakes every Christmas season, okay?"

"Oh, man. If you can't, we'll discontinue them because I'm not going to touch them with a ten-foot pole." She goes on her tiptoes to wrap me in a hug. "I'm going to miss you so much."

"I haven't been offered the job. There's no reason to miss me yet."

"Aria, they're going to hire you. And I'll have one, maybe two more good ugly-cries and then I'll be fine."

"I'm sad," I say.

"I'm sad, too. But also happy that you're spreading your wings. If you'd stayed here forever, I would have never forgiven myself for stifling you."

"It's not such a bad gig, even though you make me do that awful dance every morning."

"Hey! I'm counting on you teaching your new coworkers at the PR place that dance." Camilla clicks her tongue. "It just occurred to me that you're going to have coworkers who aren't me. You better not love them more."

"Of course I won't."

She drapes her arm around my waist and leans her head on my arm. "You ready for the festival opening? Is Theo ready?"

"Theo?" I shake my head. "I think Theo has a lot on his mind right now." I swallow down the apprehension—the almost heady, needy apprehension—I feel as I think of him. "As for me? Yes and no. Ready to wear my fancy dresses, meet and greet people, and feel the excitement in the air. Not ready for the corset. Or the possibility that it won't succeed."

"It's going to be okay," she reassures me.

It might be. All of this might be. But if Theo's not in my life anymore, for any reason, it can't.

Chapter 27

♥

Theo

The scent of cinnamon, cloves, and cranberries punctuates the air at the Barrie Mansion. The place has been totally Christmas-ified. There are dark green fabrics draped from the ceiling, and fresh evergreen garlands are tied to every inch of the banister of the grand staircase. Classical music is piped throughout the space and topiaries with gold and silver ornaments line the grand hall.

It used to be that the only good thing about Christmas in my adulthood was getting caught under the mistletoe and having to pay up. But I'll admit, begrudgingly, that somehow the festival knows how to make the season almost enjoyable.

"Hey," Aria whispers, her voice at a higher than natural pitch.

At first, I'm relieved she's not in that dark red velvet gown she wore in our promotional photo shoot. I don't think I could handle standing next to her and not reaching out to touch her waist or her glowing skin.

But it's worse than the red dress. She's wearing a white Victorian gown. The fabric has little red roses with green stems all over it. Perfect for a Christmas festival. Her hair is up in a twist. Her earrings are pearls that dangle and when she smiles, and when she tilts her head, they bob back and forth.

Beautiful.

I consider texting Jesse to make him come be my wingman, to hold me back and keep me in check so I don't do something crazy like stare at her, dumbfounded, all day.

Except, Liz and Marjorie have confiscated my phone because even the appearance of it in my pocket will "break the Victorian spell," they said.

Also, why do they and the rest of the committee get to wear those awful blazers? It's only Aria and me in period clothing. Well, and the vendors in the booths are decked out like they're extras in *A Christmas Carol*, too.

It's fine. I can be strong. If I don't let myself get distracted by the way Aria looks and smells—like a queen and juicy strawberries, respectively—I'll be fine.

But will I be okay if this whole thing fails? If sales are abysmal and booths pull out early? I know, logically, that Aria and I did everything we could to make this succeed. But somehow, I'll still feel like a failure if it fails. And what would that do to Aria?

"Did you see the crowd lined up outside?" Aria asks, her eyes darting back and forth.

I see people gathering on the front lawn of the mansion, waiting for the festival to open. Huh. "There are more people than I thought there would be, considering the near apocalypse we've been going through."

"I kept psyching myself up this morning, telling myself it's okay if there's only ten people. They'll just get lots of extra attention."

She adjusts the neckline of her dress and I about keel over at the sight of it.

"It was seriously my mantra. As long as we get ten, it's going to be okay." She sighs. "It wouldn't have been. But I was trying to prepare myself for disappointment."

I step to the long narrow windows flanking the ornate door. "You don't have to worry. There are way more than ten."

Soon, Liz, Marjorie, and Darrel open the door and security guards hold the people back as Aria and I give a quick welcome speech. People are allowed in, and we wave, smile, and greet them. The first one hundred customers to arrive get gift bags full of samples and swag, so Aria and I help pass those out.

"Can you believe the pandemonium?" I whisper to her as the line waits for a man in a wheelchair to go up the ramp.

"I am relieved. It feels like years past. There's nothing like it in all the land," she says, her gaze darting to mine before she turns and bends to say hello to a little girl, who tells Aria her dress is pretty.

"Look!" Aria spins around and the skirt swishes fast. Her head tips back in a laugh, and I'm lost in all the sensations of her.

That sight will be permanently etched into my mind.

She poses with the girl and her sister as her mom takes a photo of the three of them. "Okay, now with Theo Carter," the mom says, holding up her phone again and motioning with her hand for me to scoot closer. She leans back more. "I can't get all three of you in the shot," she says. "You're going to have to stand closer together."

Being closer to her is a glorious kind of torture. My arm is smashed between us, so Aria lifts my arm and helps it to drop around her waist so that she and I can nudge that much closer.

"Sorry to get all in your grill here, but it's for the children, so ..." she offers an apologetic smile.

A lot of the more formal Victorian dresses have necklines that are low, and Aria's is no exception, which I have a front row seat to now that I'm standing flush to her side.

I snatch my gaze back to the mom as quickly as possible.

Mercy. Aria's so beautiful.

As soon as the mom lowers her phone and thanks us, I step back and away and wave.

That interaction repeats itself multiple times for the rest of the meet and greet, as more and more people ask if they can pose for a photo with us. We even have several people ask for our autographs.

"Don't get a big head," Aria says after I sign a woman's canvas bag.

"Too late," I joke.

It's not long before Howard Beckwith, Aria's grandfather, walks through the front doors. He's in a Santa costume that hangs off his thin frame. Still, the twinkle in his eye makes him a more believable Santa figure than most around.

"Merry Christmas," he bellows, his arms wide. Pulling both of us into a hug, he laughs. "If I didn't know better, I'd think we were on a movie set of *A Christmas Carol*. You two are hawt with an 'A. W. T.'"

"It's good you're here to see it now." I say. "We don't have to be dressed up like this again until closing day. The committee is allowing us to throw on the blazers when we come here between now and then."

"Did you come to eat almonds with me, Grandpa?" Aria asks. She's beaming, her smile riveting me to the spot.

"When you're finished with the meet and greet." He looks around the room. "I'll get all my Christmas shopping done in one fell swoop."

Finally, the throngs of people have trickled to a steady, quick-moving line. We take a quick walk-through to see the booths. The committee managed to space them further apart so the fewer number of booths doesn't make the space seem sparse. We leave the back exit of the mansion and enter the tent for the remaining booths. We see Jesse and Camilla at Shorty's booth and talk with them for a while.

When we leave them to check out the remaining booths, Aria eases closer to me. I feel the heat of her arm against mine.

"What's your favorite booth, Theo?"

When I look around, trying to find something that's appealing to me, she stops us. "Oh yeah. You don't like Christmas booths."

"Okay, okay. I didn't used to like them. But I'm starting to understand their charm."

She smiles and pumps her fist. "Yes. I knew this would all pay off."

"You're invested in me liking Christmas, huh? Why?"

"I want to share what's important to me with you. You don't have to love it. I guess when something's magical to me, I can't help but want the person I care about to feel it, too."

She cares about me.

She cares about me.

Her gaze darts around and she bites her lip. "Oh, look! It's the best blankets." She rushes to the booth that houses rolls of fuzzy, silky soft blankets. She rubs her hand along several of them, lingering on the light-blue one.

"Is this your favorite booth, then?" I ask.

"That's like asking me to pick my favorite child."

"You asked *me* that question!"

"You didn't answer either."

Aria's Grandpa joins us, his shopping basket overflowing. "I'll be over there," he says, indicating the wassail stand, his brows waggling.

"Well, I'd better get over to the firm and get to work," I tell her.

"It's a Saturday," she says.

"I've got to get ready for the Fleming hearing next week."

She raises her chin. "Gotcha." She flashes a brief smile. "Well, good luck."

"Thank you." I motion throughout the crowd. "Are you planning on staying and doing some shopping?"

She only nods, offering another smile that if I'm not mistaken, might be as full of yearning as my own. Or close.

"Time to be free of the costume," I say, loosening my cravat so I can breathe.

"Theo, wait."

Aria's eyes are searching mine, and my heart starts to pound.

"I interviewed at a PR and branding firm in Highlands Ranch yesterday. They called me this morning to offer me the job. I start the beginning of the year."

I'm not prepared for this, so I revert to my go-to, the joker. "Hey! Congrats. That's really cool. That's where I graduated from high school, so maybe if you go visit the school you'll see some basketball trophies with my name on them. And some still unbroken records in cross country." I dust off my shoulder like I'm all that.

Why am I doing this? This false bravado doesn't work. It used to. But I don't like it. So why do I go there every time I feel threatened?

Maybe because Highlands Ranch is an hour away.

Taking a deep breath, I tug her close and walk her around the corner where it's quieter.

"Let me start over. Congratulations, Aria." I take in everything about her and my knees almost buckle. "But please. Please tell me how I can still see you every day. I'll move to Highlands Ranch in a heartbeat if that means I can keep sharing a wall with you."

Chapter 28

Aria

"The sun sets so early now," I say aloud as I drive on the highway heading out of Highlands Ranch. I completed all the hiring paperwork this afternoon, and my head's still full of the newness of it all—the promise of adventures that can come because I'll have a legit brand management career.

I've got my grandpa on the phone through my car's speakers. "And you're starting your new job up there in January?" he asks, his voice sounding frustrated. "That's the worst time of year to be driving on that road."

"How do you know? You're from Florida."

"The guys at the diner have educated me on the ins and outs of the weather, traffic, and politics here. I feel homegrown now."

I snort a laugh. "You even *sound* like a New Hedge old timer. Glad to hear you're acclimating to your new habitat." The dusky blue and purple sunset streams through the evergreens and pines on either side of the highway.

It's stunning. If the weather is clear, this is not a bad commute at all.

"That's me," he says. "The old gopher, digging a brand-new hole in the ground. I've convinced your mother to let me use the snow blower. Why did no one ever tell me about snow blowers before? I'd like to start a new career manning them. Do you think I'm too old to become an entrepreneur?" He pauses. "Hey! You could design the employees' T-shirts."

"I love how your mind scurries from one thing to the next without any warning. You really are an old gopher." I glance at my rear-view mirror before changing lanes. "I'd be happy to design something for you, but you'd have to print it on snow bibs because your employees are not going to wear T-shirts in the frigid air."

"Hmm. Maybe you're right. Maybe for now, I'll stick to using the snow blower on the neighbors' sidewalks for free. I'll start my business next year."

"Grandpa the dreamer. I love it." And I mean it. I think I get my rediscovered ambition from him. I chuckle as a new thought comes to mind. "Leave it to the Floridian to be the most excited one about the snow. Don't worry. It'll wear off before spring hits and you'll hate it like the rest of us."

"Never. It's gorgeous. The great equalizer. I heard the Nielsons and the Harkeys down the street don't do the best job taking care of their lawn, but with the snow piling up, no one ever knows. They should try to sell their houses in the winter."

I giggle. "Sounds like you've got everything figured out."

"I like it here. Should have moved here sooner. But anyway, back to you driving on that highway every day."

"It's not going to be every day. I only have to go into the office twice a week. I can work from home the other three."

"You mean wear your pajamas all day and eat cold cereal for lunch?"

"Is that what you would do if you worked from home?"

"Naw. I probably wouldn't bother with pajamas. I'd just stay in my boxer briefs all day."

I burst out a laugh. "Not during Colorado winters, you wouldn't. You'd freeze."

"True, true. But listen, Aria. It's great that things are already squared away for the new job. Everything happened so fast."

"I know. And during the holidays? The emergency maternity leave situation has left them scrambling. They wanted me to get started right away. I'll be doing a bunch of trainings from home after Christmas." I'm equal parts excited and unsure. It did happen fast. Still, it feels right.

"You want to come walk with me around town when I get back?" I ask him. "Not old downtown where Shorty's is, but the newer part? I'm going out again to drum up more publicity for the festival."

"You've been going out a lot. Seems like every afternoon after work."

"It's the charitable donations. That huge plastic stocking at the festival has been filling up with cash and gift cards that people have been donating, but I can't help but worry, with how crazy things have been this year, that the families we're donating to aren't going to get what they need."

"You have a kind heart," Grandpa says.

"I got it from you."

He grows quiet. "Speaking of the heart. How's the love life?"

I sigh. "I'm hanging up now."

"Wait. I promise I'm not on a secret assignment from your parents, even though they know you talk to me about this stuff."

"If they'd stop arguing or giving each other the cold shoulder for two seconds, I might be able to get a word in edgewise and tell them about this alleged love life of mine myself."

"I'll neither agree nor disagree with that statement." He clears his throat. "But really. How are things with Theo? Up and down?"

I take in the rise of mountains on either side of me, the thousands of evergreens flocked with snow casting long shadows now that the sun has nearly disappeared. "What makes you think that?"

"How else do I know about anything around here?"

I shoot out a sigh. "The guys at the diner are talking to you about me?"

"Well, I had to brag about you being my granddaughter. I saw your picture in the paper one of them was reading, you know the photo of you in that fancy English dress? Of course, I'm going to say something."

"And of course, they're going to feel it's their right to gossip about me. Great."

"They didn't say much. Just that there might be a little trouble in paradise."

"They know nothing about my life, Grandpa, okay?"

"So you and Attorney Carter are doing fine, huh?"

I groan. "I hope so." I cringe as I weigh my options. I could avoid these questions, or I can be open and honest. Suddenly, I'm so tired of dancing around the issue. I don't want to go along, doing a song and dance around my feelings. "Grandpa, I think I love him."

"My granddaughter is in love with Theo Carter, Esquire," he says, definitively. His voice is commanding and firm. For some reason, it reminds me of Theo's fake accents.

"But I can't rush into anything," I insist. "My four-year relationship ended only three months ago."

"It ended a lot longer ago than that, my dear. You two were hanging by a thread for months, maybe years."

How does he know that? I rarely spoke to him about Rob. "Did your sketchy diner gang tell you that, too?"

He gives another hearty chuckle. "No, I could hear it in your voice every time we talked."

There's another example of people around me knowing something I wasn't willing to see, or at least do anything about. "Well, even if that's the case, I'm not sure I can move forward. I don't trust that love can work out long term. People change over time and . . . I'm scared."

"Changing over time can be good. Change doesn't only have to happen in negative ways."

Frustration boils up inside me. "Things can be going along so well, can feel so right and good and then, bam, you're unhappy and the person isn't who you thought they were. Who they *said* they were."

"Then take your time. There's no need to rush."

"I took four years with my last relationship and look how that ended." My hands close tightly over the steering wheel. "I don't know how to do this love thing." I laugh, but it's bitter. "I refuse to end up like my parents. But Theo's . . . and this is going to sound strange . . . but Theo's *alive*. He's so full of life. He takes up all the space in my mind and then some. But that's sort of how Mom describes Dad . . . before they got married. Now look at them."

"It can be frightening to take risks when you've seen so many rough examples."

"Yep," I say. "It is. And I refuse to be in a relationship where there's arguing all the time. You can thank my parents for that particular life goal. I have to be opposite of them in that regard."

He sighs. "I don't know about that. Seems completely unrealistic."

"Well, I know. We can't be perfect on stuff like that. But Rob and I didn't fight. That's what I want. Zero volatility."

"And zero excitement? Geez, this isn't like you're buying a sensible beige sedan. You're finding someone you're in love with and want to be with for the rest of your life. Just because some of the people in your life, including myself, haven't managed that too well doesn't mean you can't."

"It's scary. What if I end up like my parents? No offense, since I know it's your daughter and son-in-law, but they're not happy."

"Oh, Aria. You're right. They aren't. But you feel something strong when it comes to that Theodore dude."

I laugh at his use of the name Theodore and the word "dude."

But I do. "Feeling something strong" isn't a strong enough statement.

He doesn't wait for me to respond. "And if I wish for anything for my grandkids, it's for them to not settle for the old beige sedan. I want them to be with someone that makes them come alive, someone who gives them all the feels."

I snort laugh. "Grandpa! Where did you learn that term, 'all the feels'?"

"You already know the answer to that."

I shake my head and silently thank the guys at the diner who've already taken my grandfather under their wing.

New Hedge can be a pretty decent place, and a good place to raise a family.

An ache rises in my gut. I want to raise a family of my own in my hometown.

And I want that with Theo.

Chapter 29

Theo

I'm finishing my workday by going over details of the Fleming case and drinking my fifth cup of the receptionist Charlotte's homemade, from scratch, hot chocolate. We're talking a mix of melted milk chocolate and bittersweet chocolate, a specialty vanilla milk, and a splash of heavy cream.

I'm going to hate the day when things like this hot chocolate stick to me. I still have my figure, so until then, I'm going to drink my five cups and enjoy them.

Except I probably shouldn't have because I'm not feeling so well when Weatherby walks in my office. The look of concern on his face doesn't help things, either.

"Theo," he says with a slight nod. "You have a minute?"

"I do." I straighten the piles on my desk. I figure if I can see at least forty percent of the wooden desktop, it's clean enough.

"Tell me about the Fleming case." His brow hangs low over his eyes as he eases down into the chair across from me.

Nerves zip through me, and my stomach feels worse. "I was actually working on it right now." I glance at the tab on my computer that has my notes for the case. "Court is scheduled for Friday. I'm going to meet with the client tomorrow to make sure we're good to go."

Weatherby clamps his lips together a moment. "Have you met with the prosecuting attorney?"

I nod, shifting in my seat. "I did yesterday. I think I'm seeing things differently now."

"I know criminal isn't your thing. I get it. You're a positive person, a happy guy most of the time. I can see criminal law being something you don't enjoy, and that's fine, but this case is vital to your progression in the law."

"It has challenged my perspectives, which is a good thing," I concede. "The prosecutor wants to work with us. He wants to offer probation, community service, and the completion of a year-long, once a week, mental health program for the charges to go away. If the judge will agree to that."

"Wow, that's great." Weatherby leans back in his chair, staring at me. "Do you know why I gave you this case?"

I rotate back and forth in my chair, my knee bobbing up and down a mile a minute. "You said it would round out my experience. That it would be good for me."

"Uh huh. That's true. But that's not the main reason. You needed this case to find your heart."

"What?" At the mention of the word "heart" my mind flashes to Aria. But I know he's not referring to romance or love.

"It's tough representing a criminal, especially one you don't jive with," he says. "And I know you don't jive with Marty Fleming."

"I guess I don't, but it's unethical to have that affect my job."

"I hope you're finding some things out about yourself during this process. I know a little bit about your dad." He lifts his shoulder. "Just what's on public record and I put two and two together."

At my groan, he shows me his palms. "Hey, I had to before I hired you."

"What does my dad's actions have to do with anything?"

"Your dad, well, he was known in the Denver area as something of a friend to the bad guys. He liked working with criminals, didn't he? In fact, he seemed to be all the drug dealers' favorite dude. Until he suddenly wasn't."

My chest burns. "Well, I was only five, so I didn't know at the time. But I eventually found out some of it. He ran away back east when he'd made so many enemies that it was uncomfortable for him to stick around here."

"And he left your mom, brother, and you here."

I can only nod, my chest constricting, the joints of my fingers and hands feeling weak. Tired.

"I'm not going to pretend to be able to psychoanalyze this." Weatherby's laugh is humorless. "I'm not even going to try. But this case has hit a nerve."

My mind is reeling. Before I can respond, he's out the door. He turns back around in the doorway. "Use it, Theo. Use all your personal experiences to get Fleming in the judge's good favor. Use your pain to help him," he says, before wheeling back around and returning to the main floor.

I'm stunned silent. If I'd known Weatherby was trying to orchestrate this complicated ruse of putting me on a case that would remind me of my father, I might have turned it down and taken the risk of his ire. This feels like something of a twisted game.

I crush the empty Styrofoam cup, slamming it with my fist onto my desk, drops of hot chocolate flying across it to splatter on my screen.

That felt good, for a second.

But deep down, I want nothing more than to be the person I need and want to be.

I stand from my desk, grab my laptop, and leave the office. Hopefully I'm not too late to make all this work the way it's supposed to.

Chapter 30

Theo

Dust motes circle and swirl in front of my vision. Stark white sunlight reflected off the surrounding snow-weighted giant blue spruce outside slants into the county courtroom from the bank of windows high above. The room smells of Pine-Sol and one of those air freshener plug-ins. It's a spicy apple cider and peppermint type of a scent.

Of course. Because this is the county that houses the Charles Dickens Christmas Festival. Any scent other than Christmas is poor form.

Judge Kimpton stands from her bench and gives a cursory glance over the room before being escorted out by the marshal for deliberation.

I glance at Marty, standing next to me. He's in a suit and tie, and he's got a rim around his hair again from the hat he was probably wearing right before he walked in the courthouse.

"The questions the judge asked seemed good," I offer to Marty, as the shuffling of people stretching or moving around the room gets louder. "She seems to be considering the prosecutor's plea."

He nods, blinking rapidly. "How long will we have to wait?" He shoots a glance behind us.

I know, because I looked back earlier, that several of his family members and friends are here, including Elijah.

And Aria is here, along with Camilla and Jesse.

My mom and Odin want to meet up for a meal afterwards, which was nice of them.

But Aria is here.

"I'm guessing only a few minutes," I tell Marty and clap a hand over his shoulder. "Take a drink of water." I motion to the bottle on the table in front of us. "Breathe. Maybe take a walk around the room?"

He hesitates. "I'll stay here."

He might be thinking it would be best to keep his family at arm's length. Tensions are high between them, and Marty's in a vulnerable position. They all are.

"But thanks for what you said." He rocks back and forth, clenching his jaw.

I can only nod. I don't really remember all of what I said in the closing arguments, when I pled to the judge on Marty's behalf. I know I practiced a lot beforehand, but I'm not sure I said what I'd planned.

I do know the feeling in the room, and the feelings inside of me. I tried to bring the larger picture into consideration—the kind of man Marty is, as gathered through character witness statements I'd compiled beforehand, as well as his actions before and after the theft.

He deserves a second chance, but only as it aligns with his own personal dedication to lasting recovery and change. He's just beginning to step into the road of his journey now that the truth is out there. No amount of healing can begin until truth is respected—until it's held up in the light, studied, and loved like a rare diamond.

To seek and revere truth. Maybe that's why I've gone into the law.

And maybe the judge will see fit to allow Marty to walk the dusty, winding road of recovery a free man.

At this point, I can only hope.

Hope. I glance back at Aria, and she's got a soft smile. She gives me a nod. Maybe I do know a thing or two about hope these days.

Chapter 31

Aria

I breathe in the cinnamon stick-scented air of the festival, hardly believing it's almost over.

Part of me was hoping that not being in period dress would help me be a little more anonymous at the festival, but that's not the case. Of course, the Christmas blazer is a dead giveaway.

"Aria! Hey!" A group of teens who have confidently shown up to the festival in matching cotton dresses, shawls, and white mob caps shout out to me. "Where's Theo?" one of them shouts and the rest move in closer to her in peals of laughter.

I give an exaggerated shrug and wave. It's surreal that I'm being recognized, even around town when I'm not in my blazer.

And that's a good question. Where is Theo? He only said he couldn't come, but that he would be here first thing in the morning for closing day.

I wish he could have been here. Some of the committee members and I get to extricate the money from the giant plastic stocking and take it to the bank and then go shopping for the things on the families' wish lists. We'll still be accepting donations tomorrow, Christmas Eve day, right up to the end. But the committee will be making deliveries to the families tomorrow.

I glance over the booths as I weave my way to the end near the registers. It doesn't take me quite as long as years past to make it here because at this point, we're at about seventy-five percent capacity. That means a fourth of the contracted booths pulled out of the festival.

Not ideal. The fewer booths, the less of a rich experience we offer the customers.

However, according to Camilla and Jesse, their shortbread sales haven't been hurt by this. Maybe less of a selection for the customers has helped the booths sell more. Entrance fee income has been strong, according to the committee, which is good news.

Still, my stomach is torn to shreds right now. It's the moment of reckoning. The giant stocking doesn't look at all full. If I had to guess, there's maybe half of what's normally in there. Will there be enough for the Flemings?

The court hearing went well for Marty, with the judge dropping it down to a misdemeanor. No more jail time, either. Still, Theo hasn't felt like talking much about it.

That doesn't mean I haven't been thinking about being in that courtroom with him, though. I kept to myself in the back, silent with Camilla and Jesse. But I felt permanently emotionally attached to him throughout the whole thing. It was a whole "mi casa es su casa" moment, except it was more along the lines of "your pain is my pain."

It did something to me. It sealed me to him in some way, hearing him eloquently and humbly address the judge. Humbly, yes, but like a rockstar, too. I don't know how that was possible, but Theo managed it.

I wave at Camilla, who's at her booth talking with customers as they grab items from her shelves. Marjorie is already there next to Liz at the giant plastic donation stocking, and when she sees me, she holds up the keys and jangles them. I see that a security guard is already on hand, too.

When I reach Marjorie, she leans in for a hug. "Did you hear about the storm that's supposed to come in tonight?"

"I'm not too worried. Seems like there's snow every Christmas Eve, but it never seems to affect the festival too badly."

"Well, it could affect it this year. I hear the wind is supposed to be thirty miles per hour."

We've scratched and clawed our way through these last three weeks, and it hasn't collapsed yet. It will survive one more day. I wish I knew if the Flemings will survive. I want them to have as good of a Christmas as possible.

"One of the best moments of the festival!" Marjorie cries as she helps me insert the ornery key into the lock near the base of the stocking. "No matter what the final amount is, we did our best and every bit counts. Besides, I know you were out literally knocking on doors getting more, which is admirable. Thank you, Aria."

"Where's Theo?" Liz asks. That question has been on repeat all over town.

"He's got a lot of loose ends at the firm he needs to tie up, with it being Christmas Eve tomorrow. But he'll be here for closing day."

"I don't doubt he's got work to do. I think he's the best attorney in town. He did so much to help Marty Fleming."

It feels uneasy discussing the Flemings—I wish it hadn't been so public. But Marjorie is right, Theo pulled out all the stops when working together with the judge and prosecutor for the best possible solution for Marty, and by extension, Elijah and his family.

Marjorie seems to sense that I don't want to talk about it. "In any case, the festival was made better by you and Theo. You two exude light—you're way more wholesome than Carl and Amanda." Marjorie looks ready to spit in someone's eye as she utters their names.

"I doubt Theo and I have had much to do with it, but thanks," I offer.

She holds out a narrow, magnetic sweeper. "Of course you did," she croons. "You do the honors." Marjorie glances at Liz and the security guard.

We get the bills and coins gathered into a few money bags—I notice Liz discreetly tucks several back in her bag when we see we don't need all of them—and then both Marjorie and Paul escort me to the car. He drives in his security car behind me to the bank and goes in with me as I deposit it into the festival's account.

It takes the bank teller a while to count it all, and when she gives me the amount, my jaw drops open.

"Are you sure?"

She nods. "We've had two of us count it by hand and the machine will verify. But yeah. I'm sure."

Chapter 32

Theo

The New Hedge Rec Center is teeming with people, and the noise and commotion is already giving me a headache.

I wait by the front doors, almost ready to leave and get back to my work, when I finally see him, all floppy hair and gangly arms and legs. If Marty had gone to prison, when he got back, his son would have been completely grown—well into his adulthood.

But Marty isn't going to prison.

He's not home yet, either. He's still got his other apartment. The family needs some time. And Marty's got some things to prove to the family before they feel safe to let him back in their lives. But . . . things are moving in the right direction.

I don't bother with shaking Elijah's hand when he walks in the doors. I only smile and then point to him as I tell the clerk at the front desk, "This is him."

I've paid his entrance fee—which is part of a year's pass for the whole family. But that's not something I feel comfortable divulging right now. I'll text the info for the pass to Elijah's mom later.

Elijah's expression clouds, as he warily glances from the front desk clerk back to me.

"My dad told me to meet you here."

I nod and offer a smile as I ask Elijah to follow me. We walk to the basketball courts on the far side of the center.

It's a good sign that he and his dad are speaking. At one point, Elijah, according to Marty, was refusing to speak to him. A sentiment that I remember feeling.

If my dad had ever tried to make contact, I probably would have refused it. At least I would have by the time I was a teen and my anger had solidified in my gut.

But again, I have to remember to try not to look at this through the lens of my own experiences, as much as is possible.

Marty Fleming isn't my father. Not even close. I'm relieved I finally opened my eyes to that fact before it was too late.

"How's the custodial position?" I ask Elijah.

"It's good. I get to listen to my music, and I can leave as soon as I'm done. It helps that the building's been remodeled. Everything's pretty clean as it is."

"It always looks good when I get in in the mornings."

"I heard you're the first in and the last one to leave most of the time."

"Who told you that?" It's true, but how would he know?

"I overheard Aria and Camilla."

"Aria talks about me, huh?"

Aria and I haven't seen much of each other the past couple of weeks. We've both been working nonstop, and we divide and conquer most of the time as far as the festival is concerned, trying to spread the love around.

We near the doors to the basketball courts and Elijah stops. "Thanks for helping my dad. A misdemeanor is a lot better than a felony. And bench probation's a lot better than prison. My mom thinks the community service and court-ordered therapy is going to help him the most."

I wave him off. "We can thank the prosecuting attorney for being willing to recommend all that, and the judge for accepting it."

"No, but I heard you in the courtroom. I know what you said made a difference to the judge."

A ball sticks to my throat, and I have a hard time swallowing it down.

"Elijah, your dad was saying how you had to defer your college education and that you had been signed up for a couple of sports leadership and basketball training classes."

Elijah nods, his brows knitted together.

"Now, look," I continue. "I'm not claiming to be any good. But I played in high school in Highlands Ranch and, well—" I'm nervous. It was pompous of me to have thought this was a good idea.

Elijah is chewing on the inside of his lip, and he's passing the ball back and forth in his hands.

I continue on. "I wondered if you could meet me here, maybe Tuesday and Thursday nights? I can run some drills and you can bring a couple of friends if you want. And Saturday mornings, you're welcome to join my team. We mostly just play against my brother and whoever he can scrounge up, but it's fun. Might be better than nothing since you can't take those classes right now."

"Why?"

He doesn't want pity and he really doesn't want to be a charity case. But an apology from me wouldn't hurt.

"I wanted to apologize for how I handled your dad's case at the beginning. I was letting my own biases cloud my judgement. Elijah, I guess I know how some of this feels, sort of, to have a parent struggle." I release a hot, fast breath. "Besides, the more your skills improve, the more likely it is we can beat my older brother on Saturday mornings. So really, this is selfish of me."

I don't think I imagine the slight flicker of a smile on Elijah's face before the scowl returns.

"Let's see if you can beat me," Elijah says. "I'm at least ten years younger than you, so that accounts for something."

"Ten? How old do you think I am?" I stroke the five o'clock shadow I work hard to keep at the perfect length. I've never even seen a grey hair in there. "I'd say you're no more than eight years younger. You're eighteen, right?"

"Still," Elijah starts dribbling between his legs in a figure eight pattern, never taking his eyes off mine. "I'm in my prime and you're on a downhill slope. So, we'll see."

I can't stop the huge grin that splits my face. "Bring it."

And he does. For the next hour and a half, Elijah's basketball skills reduce me to a sweating, air-sucking mess. I'm not used to playing against someone with as much endurance as he has. Man, my friends from the team are totally out of shape. And, okay, so am I. Maybe I really should cut back on those thick hot chocolates Charlotte makes.

We finish right as the rec center announces over the PA system that they're closing in fifteen minutes.

"Your dad wasn't kidding," I say, out of breath. "I think I've learned more from you than you have from me."

Elijah acquiesces. "You're a better ball handler than I am, I'll give you that. But you have a funny shot. That thing is just . . . ugly." He laughs and then, in between dribbles as we head down the hall, he gives me a shove.

"Me? I was thinking the same thing about yours. I've got to cure you of that disgusting form."

"We'll see," Elijah says, and by now, his smile lights up his whole face.

"So? Thursday night? After your custodial shift?" I ask him after I finish sucking up what feels like a gallon of water from the drinking fountain.

"I'll try." He doesn't meet my gaze when he tells me thanks.

The wind bites into me, even through my coat as I walk to my car in the rec center parking lot. The snow is pelting my windshield on my drive home, and I wonder if I'm going to make it without sliding off the road. I hope Elijah makes it safely home in his compact sedan.

Chapter 33

Aria

I arrive home to my apartment and strip off my protective gear, hanging the dripping mess of gloves, hat, and double puff coat in my bathroom to dry out. It's near blizzard conditions out there, which I both love and hate. I love the snow, and I hate the hazards it can cause.

Once I'm in my snowman-print, long underwear-style pajamas, I make myself a cup of hot cocoa and retire to my room.

Yes. I'm in my bedroom in the hopes of hearing Theo next door. If he's there, I'll knock on the wall.

I miss him.

The gifts that the members of the committee and I spent hours buying tonight are safely stowed in a secure, private location. We have to keep the thousands of dollars' worth of food, toys, clothing, gift cards, and household items safe. But I had to laugh when we pulled into the maze of storage units across from Shorty's.

Ah, the irony. The place that bothers me so much is actually coming in handy for a change.

Still, nothing was purchased for the Flemings. In past years, the donations reached in the tens of thousands of dollars. Barely any of it actually made it to the families.

Even so, this year's smaller amount feels like a failure. It stings. I'd really hoped my pounding the pavement and all the efforts of everyone involved would have pushed us over the edge. But the families that Santa's Helpers had agreed to help previously got first priority. Makes perfect sense, but what's the Flemings' Christmas going to look like? Will their own stockings be empty?

Santa's Helpers will be making the deliveries to the families tomorrow, while Theo and I spend the last day at the festival. A rush of heat hits me as I think of Theo in his Victorian wear. Who would have ever thought this modern young professional would look so stunning in a cravat and frock coat?

And more than that, my heart softens as I think of Theo himself, how he worked with the prosecuting attorney to convince the judge to give Marty Fleming bench probation instead of prison time, which means he's not even required to have a probation officer.

Seeing Theo in that courtroom? Everything in me hummed with love for him as I saw him defend Marty Fleming with power and compassion.

He also got Elijah the custodial job at the firm.

His work co-hosting a Christmas festival when his own memories of Christmas haunt him has been selfless.

And the way he looks out for me and takes care of me makes my stomach flutter.

When my cup of cocoa is nearly gone, I hear it. A rustle through the wall. It could either be Elijah doing his custodial job or Theo. I wait, and when I hear someone clearing his throat exactly like Theo does, I hazard a light knock and press my ear to the wall.

"Aria." He says it in soft surprise. I love the way my name sounds on his lips, even through the muffle of an old wall.

"Hey."

"Hello." I can hear the smile in his voice. "How did the shopping with the committee go tonight?"

"It was a lot of fun." I swallow hard. "I missed you."

He breathes a grunt of happiness. "I missed you, too. I wish I could have been there. I had to drive over to Denver today, and then I met up with Elijah at the rec. Now I'm finishing up some things so I can enjoy the holidays."

"*Enjoy* the holidays? That hasn't happened before, has it?" My tone is soft. Where once my tone might have been dismissive or even frustrated about him not liking Christmas, I get it now.

"No. It's amazing what being in love can do to one's perspective."

I inhale, soaking it all in.

Theo Carter is in love with me.

"Can I sledgehammer this wall right now?" I laugh. "Theo? I love you, too." Now I'm plastered to the wall like a starfish, or those gummy toy sticky hands that kids throw at hard surfaces. Must be as close to him as possible. I'm about to be a mess on the floor, so dizzy in love I can't stand up anymore.

"Why is it kind of cool that we first said those words through a wall?" he asks.

"It's certainly unique. I kinda like that."

My phone dings with a text. An ALL-CAPS message to the entire committee from Liz Langer, complete with asterisks and exclamation points. Several of them.

I gasp when I read it. "Theo, did you see the text from Liz?"

A moment later, he gasps, too. "A tree smashed through the roof of the Barrie Mansion?"

Tomorrow is the last day of the festival and for this to happen now, at nearly eleven o'clock the night before, is awful.

Okay, enough talking through the wall, I'm dying to see him. We have to discuss this tragic event in person.

But he beats me to it.

"Want to go check it out with me?"

Chapter 34

♥

Theo

I meet Aria at the back entrance of Shorty's, and as she steps out in the wind and snow, I cover her head with an industrial strength umbrella. There's no way I'm going to let her get pelted with ice as she walks to my car, but I fight with the umbrella. The wind is crazy.

She's in long underwear and UGG boots, which I got to see before she yanked on her coat as we left. Why does this woman torture me like this? The thin fabric hugs her every curve, and her thick dark hair is piled high atop her head in a messy bun. Which is sexy, especially because I can better see her face.

Before I open the passenger side door, I prop the umbrella above us to protect us from the storm, then lean in for a kiss. She parts her lips, and we linger there, our foreheads pressed together, warm in the cold air.

Once in the car, I drive, and Aria helps me navigate through the thick snowfall to get to Barrie Mansion. The powder is relentless, but the real culprit is the wind. The drifts are blowing across the road, making visibility low.

Finally, we make it.

I ease the Beemer to a stop in the parking lot across the street from the mansion.

"Oh my—" Aria slaps her hands over her cheeks as she surveys the damage. A large branch from an old oak, the giant that has graced the property for several decades, has torn away from the tree and crashed through the roof. The top section of an upper floor wall has been ripped away, as well. Emergency crews, bundled up from head to toe to protect them from the elements, are on the scene with a backhoe and a tractor. The house is dark.

We approach the open front doors and are stopped by a guy in an orange reflective vest over his snow gear. "This area is closed now," he says, holding up a hand.

Aria and I glance at each other.

"Is it unsafe inside?" I ask him.

"No. We just don't want the general public—" He stops and steps closer to us, seeing us in the flashing lights of the emergency vehicles. "Oh. You're Aria and Theo."

I nod as Aria says, "Yes. We needed to assess the damage ahead of tomorrow's closing day."

"Of course. I didn't realize who you were." His voice is apologetic. He gestures to the grand staircase in the main lobby. "They're asking everyone to stay out of the top floor, but you're welcome to have a look around the main floor. And be careful. The fire marshal is around here somewhere. I'm sure he can answer any questions you might have."

The three of us step inside and I point to the chandelier above us. "The power is out, huh?"

He frowns. "The tree branch crashed through a powerline. It's going to be a while until we can get the electrical up and running."

"A while? As in several hours?" Aria asks, lines creasing her forehead.

"I'd say a couple of days, minimum."

Aria's expression clouds, but we thank him and walk further in, using our flashlights to help us make our way through the rows of booths.

"That was kind of a trip. Sometimes it's advantageous to be the co-hosts," I say to her as I guide her so we can maneuver around a corner.

She doesn't say anything as I shine a light on the ceiling directly below where the tree damage is.

"Doesn't seem to be leaking anywhere," I say.

We make our way through the booths in the main living area—the most prime of the festival real estate where booth owners have paid a premium for their spot—and into the grand ballroom, where the bulk of the booths are.

"It's like we're in a bad dream," Aria says, shining her flashlight on darkened corners and rows of quiet merchandise. "Tomorrow's the last day. Even though it's shorter since it ends at two o'clock, it's usually one of the most profitable in revenue."

She slows her step, sucking in a breath.

I squint to read the sign she's looking at. "The candied almond stand?" The booth's roll top is closed, but the scent in the air is unmistakable.

"Grandpa and I never got any this year. We meant to, but his basket was so full when he was here that we decided to wait. We were going to tomorrow." One corner of her mouth perks up, but then she frowns again. "It's not a big deal, but I'll be sad if we don't get the chance."

I fight to know what to say, settling for a soft, "I'm sorry," as I drape my arm around her shoulders.

"Maybe we should break in and grab a couple bags of the honey vanilla kind," she jokes. "We could leave some money for them."

She offers a laugh, but it ends in a choking sob. She covers her face with her hands. "This is silly of me," she says, her words muffled by her hands. After a moment, she raises her head. "At least the festival happened. At times, we weren't sure it even would. Still, I'll be sad if closing day has to be cancelled."

My arm tightens around her. How do I do this? How do I help the woman I love? If I thought it would help, I'd totally break into the booth and snag a bunch of almonds. But the point is to enjoy them with her grandpa. Here.

We continue on, my arm slipping from her, the weight between us growing as we illuminate the shadows of the rest of the booths. I know she has things to say, stories to tell me of all of these booths, these tiny pieces of her childhood. We come to a stop at the trainset and village, the largest one of its kind that I've ever seen. Aria's face is grim.

"It looks so different in the dark," I say.

She only tilts her phone at an angle so she can better see it. Without a word, she keeps walking along the booths, her UGGs making a slight squeak with every step. She's silent, though, and I am, too.

Reaching the double wide back door adjacent to a large, old kitchen, we stand at the window, surveying the snow being blown sideways in the fierce gusts.

"Theo?" Aria clutches the window frame. "They're not going to let people in here tomorrow, are they?"

I blow out a slow breath. "Honestly, probably not." I face her and brush away a strand of hair that's escaped her bun. "I can't wrap my head around not having a closing day. There's got to be something we can do."

"Theo." Grief carves through her features. "I'm sad about the Flemings. About everything."

I can't fix this. This storm, this act of God, is beyond my control. I'd give anything to make it right. And I know this isn't my fault. But I hurt for Aria's hurt.

The woman I love is hurting, and there's nothing I can do about it.

Chapter 35

♥

Theo

We weave our way back out to the front entrance, waving half-heartedly to the guy in the orange reflective vest.

No. This isn't going to work. I have to fix this.

"Would it ever work to move locations somehow, Aria?" I open the umbrella and pull her tighter to me, taking in a sharp breath as the wind hits our faces.

She gives me an incredulous look, and I don't even let her answer that. "Of course it wouldn't. The logistics of that would be . . ." Dumb idea. Besides, there isn't another location in New Hedge even remotely large enough.

Things go from bad to worse as we see a cascade of streetlamps go out, with a zip, the lamps, one-by-one, fizzle in a line all the way up and down the road the mansion is on.

"Okay, more of the power is gone now," I state the obvious. "Must be an overloaded transformer."

Now her jaw is so hard, she'd have a hard time opening her mouth to speak, even if she wanted to.

"Um, maybe we could have the vendors bring wagons or carts and they can sell their items up and down the town center tomorrow?"

"The weather, Theo. It's too cold, not to mention the snow and wind."

As if on cue, some reflective emergency equipment that we're passing flips on its side in a gust of wind, sliding to a stop near our feet.

I tighten my grip on her. We're almost to the BMW and then we can be safe and warm inside while we figure out what to do.

A chill whips through me, but it's not the wind.

It's fear.

I've set up this festival, maybe even this Christmas in general, to mean something for our relationship, a representation that somehow, against the odds, we can make it possible. That we can make a seemingly impossible situation flourish and grow into a meaningful thing, a lasting thing.

And I might be dramatic or out of touch right now, but that fear is present. The fear that if the festival is ending in failure, that somehow means me and Aria will.

Once we're safe inside the car and warming our frozen fingers, I ask Aria how she's doing, not sure I want to hear the answer.

"The festival is just the festival, right? It's not what Christmas is actually about." She shrugs, flicking a tear off her cheek with her fingernail. "And it happened. It didn't end in the way we wanted it to, but at least it happened."

"Yeah. And despite the lower number of booths, it seems like the vendors are happy with how things turned out."

She stares at me.

"What?" I ask.

She chuffs, and it comes out like a mix between a laugh and a revelation.

"Follow me," she pulls her coat hood up and opens the passenger door. Before I can say a word, she's tumbled out of the car and is running, a saunter with high knees, in the snow back to the mansion, her boots getting lodged in a drift every few steps.

I struggle to catch up, abandoning any hope I can open the umbrella while I'm running. I catch up to her once we're inside and she's winding her way through the rows of booths again, this time at a rapid pace. She pushes through the back door and goes out under the canopy walkway towards the darkened event tent.

She holds her flashlight high, her head whipping in every direction as she takes in the layout of the tent. Finally, she meets my gaze. "I think this might actually work."

"If you can get two of them loaded up and over here, that would be even better," I tell my friend over the phone. He agrees and I hang up, making my way around a generator to reach Aria, who's plugging in a heat lamp the size of a freeway sign.

She stands and though she seems tired, an enormous grin lights up her face.

"Any luck?"

"That was Steve. He's bringing over two forklifts, and another friend who is also certified is coming to drive the other one."

She looks around at the empty back half of the event tent and rubs her gloved hands together. "Hallelujah. And I don't even want to know what time it is. But can you believe this?" She gestures around the room as committee and community members walk in the tent carrying portable heaters, extension cords, and generators.

Merre appears, her knitted cap covered in snow. "I cleared out Walmart. Bought every can of propane they had."

"Merre?" Aria hugs her. "Thank you. How did you hear about this?"

"I've been obsessing over the town's Instagram lately. People make the funniest comments. Anyway, someone posted about the tree crashing through the roof and how everyone should come to help." She shrugs. "We can't let the festival end so unceremoniously, right? Oh!" She reaches in her pocket. "I have a few portable cellphone chargers, too. Hopefully that helps."

Someone claps me on the shoulder, and I turn to see Weatherby and his wife each holding a large box.

"Battery-powered candles. Do you think you can use them?" Weatherby asks.

"Man, this is a sight for sore eyes," I say as I look over the box. "Thank you."

"You can thank my wife. She hopped on Facebook right before bed and saw your post in the community group. We're here to help, Theo."

"How's the storm? Seems better but it's hard to tell inside the tent."

"It's letting up if you can believe it. And I heard some of the city workers are already up driving the snowplows to make sure people can still get here in the morning."

I introduce them to Aria and then they leave to get to work, placing the candles all around the room on the booth's counters. We're going to need as much light as we can get for this harebrained scheme of ours.

Aria nestles herself into my arms. "As soon as those forklifts come, that's when the real work will start."

"But we're doing it, Aria. We're making this a reality. It's going to be an amazing experience. I'm so glad you thought of it."

"Thank you. For all of this. For everything." She seals a kiss to my cheek. "You've fought like a dragon for this festival, just like you said you would."

Camilla and Jesse arrive. They begin closing up the booths inside, readying them to be transported.

The plan is to move all the booths set up inside the mansion—over one hundred of them—to the event tent. And here's a silver lining to having fewer booths participating this year: the tent ended up being only half-full, which means, hopefully, we can cram all of the ones from the mansion inside it.

And with any luck, the surprise I have planned for tomorrow will help Aria have the best Christmas she's ever had.

Chapter 36

Aria

Four a.m.

Throughout my life, I've only done a few things at 4 a.m. besides sleep. Once I had the stomach flu and puked at four a.m. That's a lovely memory.

Another time, I took a redeye to New York, and we had a layover in Atlanta, so I'm pretty sure at four a.m. that day I was chugging caffeine in every form I could find, trying not to fall asleep until we boarded for the last leg.

And last night? At four a.m., Theo and I, with a lot of help from forklift operators and community members helping transport the goods by hand, secured the last booth from inside the mansion to the tent outside.

And without a speck of caffeine in me to boot. With the adrenaline that comes when you decide to do something as crazy as that, we didn't need any.

As it always does in an emergency, New Hedge came together. And now, after about three hours of sleep, I'm rushing around my apartment in a state of confusion, willing my fuzzy head to start operating at a level that will allow me to get dressed, in Victorian dress, no less, and make it over to the opening of the closing day—the beginning of the end.

Camilla comes upstairs to do my hair, finding more patience to do the ringlets around my hairline than I could ever muster, even on a day where I'm not sleep deprived.

She drives me to Barrie Mansion—she got more sleep than I did—and we stare at the wreckage as we pull up.

"It looks better in the daylight," Camilla offers.

I can't look away from the historical treasure, built at the beginning of the twentieth century, looking so torn up. Caution tape lines the entire pathway around the mansion. Makeshift boards have been secured to the roof to keep out the elements until a lasting fix can go in. It's a pock on the beautiful, red brick masterpiece. Plywood covers the hole in the wall upstairs that the branch made, which is scattered in pieces in the snow on the front lawn, piles of sawdust littering the otherwise pristine white blanket. The maintenance crew has shoveled a walking path through the snow around to the back so people can avoid entering the mansion altogether.

"This is so sad," is all I can utter.

Camilla pulls over near the makeshift path. "I'll drop you off here. You don't need to try to walk through the parking lot in your red velvet dress and satin flats."

I make my way around the back of the property to the tent, heartened by the lines already forming outside and the greetings from people who know me personally or recognize me as the face of the festival.

The face of the festival. It's been a wild ride. And the best thing to come of it is my love—soul deep—of Theo.

I enter the tent, nice and cozy, thanks to the extra generators and heat lamps we gathered throughout the night. There are even bits and pieces of the décor from inside the mansion to brighten things up in here. Although, I don't think it's necessary. The booths and the people in them do that job well enough.

"Aria, I'm glad you're here." One of the volunteers at the makeshift front desk area smiles, her nose a sharp pink. "Be sure to let people know we're still taking last-minute donations in the big stocking if people are so inclined."

"Sure," I nod.

As I turn to station myself at the entrance, there's Theo, in his frock coat and Victorian boots. It feels too long since I've seen him, even though it's only been a few hours. It's no longer snowing, but the sky is overcast—a dull white. In the dim light of the tent, his features are strong, the line of his shoulders making me stare.

"How do you look like you slept eight hours last night?" I ask him as I pull him into a hug.

"I don't think you're seeing clearly," he says, his warmth engulfing me.

"You could be right. I have blinders on when I look at you." I push him to arm's length, soaking him in. "All I see is the guy who spent his entire night making this whole thing work."

"We pulled it all together. You and me."

"I like the thought of you and me," I tease, glancing at his lips. I wish I could ravish his lips here and now, but this is a family friendly event . . . and we've had enough scandals around here.

Although, on second thought, if kissing him causes a scandal . . . I'll be a rebel all day long.

We move apart when I hear someone's phone taking a photo of us. Great.

The woman giggles as she lowers her phone. "I couldn't help it. You're so cute together."

The friend next to her laughs. "That was some good staring. I'm going to tell my husband to ogle me like that."

We greet people for the next couple of hours, recommending at times that they be sure to stop by Shorty's booth, and if they're so inclined, to contribute to Santa's Helpers on their way out.

The crowds don't let up, but I only have eyes for Theo.

I'm an independent woman. With the utmost respect, I throw my hands up at Beyonce, because I'm a honey making money. And soon, with my new position at Wolfe Strategies, I'll be a mama who profits dollars, no doubt.

But right here, right now? I'm with Theo, who I'm falling for—deeply, irrevocably, madly. And he's in very nice, Victorian slacks and a Mr. Darcy shirt.

Didn't men's fashion move slow enough back then that Mr. Darcy's white shirt would still be in circulation in some form during the Victorian period? I don't know, but I'm choosing to go with that.

It comes time for us to disperse amongst the crowds and mingle. And for me to get out of this corset. "I brought some other clothes, so I'm going to go change," I tell Theo.

"Let me guess. Your blazer?"

I answer him with a smile. "And I'm going to brush out the ringlets and remove the dozens of bobby pins that are poking me in the head."

"Aw, I like the ringlets." He sighs. He brings his hand up to tug gently on one of my curls near my low bun.

His Mr. Darcy shirt has inched to one side so that I can see the smallest part of his chest—the strong muscles and taut skin. The effect of it weakens my ankles.

"Aria, I need to go. There are a few things I need to wrap up. But can I come by and pick you up later?"

"Sure. I'm staying until the very end. I think my grandpa and siblings will be coming by a little later."

"Enjoy that." His smile is triumphant and proud. Like he's proud of me.

"I will."

He tugs me to him and kisses me.

I no longer care about the crowds.

Theo's grinning as he helps me along the pathway from the festival at two o'clock. The storm is over. I even see some patches of blue sky to the north.

"There was some more money from today at the bottom of the donation stocking," I tell Theo as we're hand in hand. I feel so watched over by him. And handholding? It's totally underrated.

"And it's for the Flemings, right?"

"Yes, Liz and Marjorie are going to take it over to them in a bit. Straight cash. No time to buy anything special. It's a shame they can't buy some nice things for them, but maybe giving them the money is best."

We cross the street and into the parking lot. As we near a large van, Theo unlocks it and opens the door.

"Milady." Theo motions to get in.

"Traded in the Beemer?" I ask as I climb up into the seat.

"Borrowed it for the day. The Beemer is safely in my garage."

"I don't know what you've got planned, but this seems safer to drive in the snow anyway."

"Maybe," he says with a shrug. He's purposely avoiding my gaze, and I get a thrill wondering what this is all about.

It's not until we're driving down the road that I hear things sliding around the back. I turn to see several boxes and bags.

"Were you Christmas shopping today?"

He keeps his eyes on the road. "I was. But don't ask me any more questions."

"Is all that stuff back there for me?"

"I said no more questions." He bumps out a laugh.

I giggle, too. What is Theo cooking up?

When we pause at a stoplight, he faces me. "I heard it on good authority that your family Christmas Eve stuff won't start until later, like seven. So I was wondering if I could spend some time with you?"

"You better," I tease. "These past couple of weeks have been busy."

"Yes, and I'm sorry about that. How about I drop you off at your apartment so you can rest for a bit? And then dinner? Can I please cook for you?"

My stomach is ravenous. "Please, please feed me. Except I'm not too tired, surprisingly. I don't want to rest." I feel like a toddler refusing to take a nap.

He snickers. "I have something else I need to do. It won't take long."

"And I can't come with you?" There's a console between us in this van. If there weren't, I'd sidle up to him and nuzzle him, begging him to stay nearby.

"It won't work if you do." His mouth twitches, holding back a smile. "Trust me."

I cross my arms. "Alright. I'll try to be patient."

We arrive at Shorty's, and it's closed for the holiday. He escorts me upstairs and I unlock my door. Before I step through, he wraps an arm around my waist and presses a kiss to my forehead. "I'll see you soon. Go lie down, okay?"

"Maybe for like twenty minutes." Fatigue hasn't hit me yet. Spending the day soaking everything up has taken care of that. But still, I'm afraid if I lie down, I'll be dead to the world, and that won't do. I want to spend every moment I can with Theo.

I pad back to my room and shrug off the blazer, dropping it on the desk chair. I'm not motivated enough right now to hang it up. Easing onto the bed, I wrap my arms around one of my several pillows and close my eyes.

Moments, or maybe hours later, I'm dreaming of Theo on the bed next to me, whispering sweet nothings.

"Knock, knock. Aria?"

I startle awake. He's not here, but his voice is. I sit up and scoot close to the wall. "Theo?"

"Did I wake you?"

"Maybe," I say around a yawn.

"Oh, I'm sorry. You said twenty minutes and I gave you forty. Lie back down and then let me know when you want to get up."

I fan my hands out against the wall. "Theo, no. I want to be with you."

There's a long pause, and then he laughs. "Go out onto the balcony, then."

I scramble out of bed, raking my fingers through my hair. Is seeing him several feet away better than not at all?

I guess so.

When I open the door, the first thing I notice is that someone—a hundred bucks says it's Theo—has shoveled the snow off my balcony. The next thing I see?

"A dumbwaiter?" I gaze at the rope and pulley system that goes from my balcony to his.

"It's a pulley clothesline, but yeah, we can call it a dumbwaiter if we want." His face is animated as he tugs on the rope to bring the dark brown, woven basket closer to him.

"You made this today?" I stammer. "How?"

"A couple of carabiners. Some rope. A clothesline tightener." He shrugs. "And Camilla's key so I could get in your apartment."

"Thank goodness I cleaned my room last night," I say, and then slap my hand over my mouth. I can't help but laugh as I grasp the rope and pull to bring the basket closer to me.

"Now, wait a moment." He stops the movement of the rope with his hands. "I need to pass you something first."

"Is it you? Maybe you can climb in the basket since it's bigger than I'd imagined."

He throws his head back in a laugh. "I'm happy you want me over there. But close your eyes."

I squeeze them shut, and I know I have the goofiest smile on my face. I hear the rope rubbing against the carabiners and when the basket bumps up against my railing, I squeal. "Can I open them?"

"Yes, you can." Theo's across the way, leaning on the railing, a sloppy grin on his face. The way he's looking at me? Well, let's just say I feel like I could fly right over to him, like a partridge or a turtle dove.

And the second thing that catches my eye? A thick, silky, fuzzy baby-blue blanket. "Did you get this from the festival? It's the one I wanted." I lift it from the basket and wrap it around myself, rubbing my cheek against the soothing softness.

We stare at each other, roughly six feet apart in our matching balconies. I can't believe it's Christmas Eve and I get to be with the man I love, the man who's done so much for me, and for my heart.

I give him one last look before stepping back into the apartment, clanging down the steps, and out Shorty's front door, the blanket still wrapped tightly around me. The firm's door isn't locked, so I race inside and up the steps to Theo's office. I'm on the balcony and in his arms, nearly knocking him off balance. That would not have been a good thing considering we're two stories up.

"Thank you." I breathe in his masculine, minty scent, losing myself as I cling to him.

Please. I don't want to let go of him ever again.

"Merry Christmas, Aria," he whispers against my hair.

I wrap the blanket around him so it's covering both of us. "The blanket's huge."

"I bought the biggest one they had so we could share it sometimes." He kisses me on the cheek near my nose, then brushes a thumb where his lips were. "The most appealing sprinkle of cinnamon freckles I've ever seen," he breathes as if in awe.

I dip my head and then return his gaze. "I'm partial to the gold and mahogany flecks in those blue eyes of yours, myself." My fingertips drift from his waist to his lithe back and I can't help but explore the muscles, taking in the lean, sculpted lines. I could touch them the rest of the day and into next week.

"Mahogany? I've never heard that about my eyes before."

"Oh, I've dreamt up entire worlds where those eyes of yours are concerned, Theo."

He chuckles and tightens his grasp. After a moment of relishing in the warmth of him, he whispers in my ear. "Do you want to go doorbell ditching with me when it gets dark?"

"Uh. Not what I was expecting you'd say. But . . . sure?"

He pauses, then whispers. "I got a bunch of things for the Flemings, but I want to keep it anonymous."

"Theo! That's amazing—"

"It wasn't all me." He rubs my arms under the blanket. "An organization of attorneys throughout the state donated. They stepped up at the last minute. I only had to go into Denver to pick up the funds and then get the items."

"Which is why you had to leave the festival early?"

"That and the dumbwaiter, which I'm excited to keep using. I'm going to spoil you with that thing, Aria."

"Me, too. I want to spoil you. And you're helping the Flemings even more than you already have. Thank you, Theo."

"I want to do all I can."

I pull him tighter. "You are a dream come true."

He kisses me, first on my cheeks, then chin, then lips. When we're breathless, I let go. I have to look in his eyes again.

His gaze has met my own, and those blue pools ask me things I could never answer with words.

"Theo." It's one word, but maybe, with any luck, he'll understand what saying his name does to me.

"I love you, Aria." His gaze feasts on every inch of my face, drinking me in.

I crush him in a kiss, more forcefully than I'd planned. His lips—and everything about him and everything he is—send me soaring. I pull back only to see his face, to touch his cheeks and jaw. "I love you, Theo."

I kiss him again and again, until he whispers against my lips. "Let's play Toenails."

I laugh. I know what he means. If we don't stop now, I'll be tempted to cancel Christmas and kiss him for days to come.

"The tiebreaker? You are so on."

The End

Epilogue

Aria

One year later

Dark, ominous clouds slide across my vision in the distance as I drive to the last day of the Charles Dickens Christmas Festival. It's the morning of Christmas Eve, and in lieu of Victorian dress, I convinced the committee to allow Theo and I to wear our Christmas blazers.

Not that I don't love me some Victorian clothing. But with all the work he and I have been doing this past year, the committee was none too happy to grant me this wish. I needed a reprieve from the stays, corsets, and especially the ringlets.

Because I'm a little tired. My job at Wolfe Strategies has been amazing, but it's not easy. So, slipping on the blazer feels like a comforting, well-deserved treat after a long day. A long year.

Although, when Theo got word yesterday that we didn't have to dress up, he looked oddly unhappy. What has come over my sweet, sweet man?

He's my man.

Mine.

And I'm as proud and giddy because of it as I was last year. Even more so.

I pull into the parking lot at the Barrie Mansion and claim the spot with a placard sporting my name. We were granted an official parking spot when we told them we were coming back as co-hosts this year.

I'm out of my car and into the mansion just as lines of customers start forming a few minutes before we open the doors. The whole place smells like wassail and cranberries. Fresh evergreen boughs adorn every possible surface of the mansion. The vendors and their booths seem ready to go. It's a gorgeous sight, one that I'm thankful for, as last year's closing day, which we unexpectedly spent in the tent in the back, replays in my mind.

In the grand foyer, I sense him, or maybe even smell his spicy scent, just before he slides his arms around my waist and buries his head in my hair.

"Good morning," Theo says, nuzzling into me a little more. "You ready for this?"

I relish his arms around me, closing my eyes. "I am. Are you? I can't believe another festival is in the books."

"Well, almost in the books. You never know what could happen."

I spin around and pin him with a look. "Don't. Remember last year?" I shudder as I think of the broken tree branch debacle, staying up all night, working on moving a hundred booths from the broken and dark mansion.

"I do. But everything always turns out in the end."

I clasp his hands in mine, right before Liz Langer moves to unlock the doors so we can begin. "My eternal optimist."

"I have been thinking about—" he hesitates, letting his gaze drop to the floor before brightening in a smile. "Well, I've been thinking about this year. Everything last year felt like an uphill climb. This time around? It's been a lot smoother."

"You up for year three?" I ask, my eyebrows waggling.

"You can't ask me that until New Years is over. At least. I'm tired."

"Me, too. How do all these committee members do it year after year?"

"I think it gets in your blood," he says, gently tugging on a lock of my hair. "Sort of like what you've done to me."

Before I can respond, Liz opens the door.

"You can't say stuff like that when I don't have time to savor it." I rise to meet him in a quick kiss. "But I'll be thinking of it all day."

I grasp his hand as long as I can before we pull apart, a necessity as Liz is funneling everyone in our direction.

We wave and greet, and before I know it, it's time for us to tend to the other duties of the day, a million tiny odds and ends.

Theo and I are at the homemade soap booth, helping the vendor pass out samples of oatmeal and honey soaps, when I hear Grandpa Beckwith's "Ho, ho, ho!" Decked out in a Santa costume, he's stuffed his middle with who-knows-what to add a paunch he doesn't have. He's even got a furling, fluffy, fake beard on.

"Grandpa! I love it."

His eyes widen. "*Grandpa?* You deign to pretend the great Santa Claus of the North Pole is your grandfather?" He reaches me and leans in to whisper. "We can't have the little ones thinking I'm an imposter."

"Oops." I whisper back. I giggle and straighten to shake his hand. "Welcome to the festival, Santa. I hope as our esteemed guest, you'll find everything in top-notch order."

He winks and mouths "Well played," before continuing in the line of people with more "Ho, ho, ho's."

"What gave him that idea?" I ask Theo.

"He mentioned what a shame it was that there was no Father Christmas here and decided to take it upon himself," Theo says with a laugh.

"Wow! That man is full of surprises."

"He's thriving here in New Hedge, isn't he?" Theo says, the edges of his eyes crinkling.

It's touching that he cares about my grandfather. He cares about my whole family, and I don't know, but something about his presence in our lives has seemed to soften my parents some. It's a nominal amount, but it's something.

And it was good for all involved when Grandpa moved out of my parents' house in the spring and into the basement apartment of one of his friends from the diner. He even started helping with the cheesecakes at the bakeshop every morning. We have so much fun, it's almost criminal...it doesn't feel like a job to be working there with him and Camilla every morning the past couple of months.

I mill around, at various times losing track of Theo only to have him show up again. The busyness of closing day consumes me, so much so that I barely have any time to grab the bite of lunch that was brought us committee members and left in a back room.

Just as it's nearing two o'clock and things are winding down, I hear Marjorie Clements' voice over the intercom. "Please gather in the grand foyer for a presentation by Father Christmas."

A presentation by Father Christmas? What is that all about?

What has Grandpa done now?

I rush out of the tent, through the back of the mansion, and as I round the corner near the entrance, I see Grandpa in that ridiculous beard, sitting on a red and gold, classic Santa throne near a wide column. Is he going to have kids sit on his knee?

People are gathering around, and I see so many that I know and love, like Camilla, Jesse, Merre, and several committee members. Theo isn't here, though. The talking is hushed as Grandpa starts a speech.

"The merriest of Christmases to you all," he begins, enjoying the attention as only Howard Beckwith can. "There are a couple of people here who I know will have a most memorable and meaningful Christmas, so I'm going to let them have the floor."

I don't have time to process what he's said, as Theo steps from behind the column. He's wearing his Christmas blazer—that tacky, gorgeous thing—and he's holding a bouquet of deep red roses.

"Aria." He meets my gaze from across the room. "Please?" His eyes plead with me to join him. I realize my hands have covered my mouth and I'm frozen to the spot.

I jolt to attention and walk towards him, shaking my head as my smile grows. He hands me the bouquet and I bury my nose in it, inhaling its sweetness. Over the flowers, I see my siblings and parents, as well as Theo's mom and stepdad, Odin. My jaw drops open and tears prick my eyes at their wide smiles.

I know what's happening and I can't wait to give him my answer.

"Aria, I think a part of me has loved you since the moment our eyes met at Shorty's bakeshop over three years ago," he says, one arm around my waist.

"Yeah, Shorty's!" Merre hoots.

We all laugh.

"Sometimes I still kick myself that I didn't handle things better in that moment. I think, if I'd only been kinder and more respectful, I might not have wasted so much time living without you. But then I remember that in life, we're not behind or ahead. Things are just right. Things work out exactly the way they were meant to. And now, you're here with me. And we look like we work in a department store in our blazers."

"Hey!" I protest before briefly slapping a hand over my face.

The twinkle in his eye nearly upends me, but I force myself to breathe. I want to take this all in, to remember every part of this.

"I almost asked you to change into your Victorian velvet gown and I'd put on my frock coat for this." He lifts a shoulder. "But, alas." His voice goes higher as he slides into a British accent. "I think this is even better."

"You know if you want me in your life, you need to get used to the blazer," I tell him, straightening the lapel.

He nods and smiles. "Oh, I am. Santa? We're ready for our gift," he says to Grandpa, who's already standing and pulling out a large, decorative fabric bag from behind his throne.

Grandpa joins us, reaches in the bag and pulls out a gold box with a white ribbon tied around it.

It's a small box.

Theo takes it from him and drops to one knee. My eyes sting again, and I blink away tears.

"Aria Robinson. My love. My life. I almost said something earlier when you mentioned my eternal optimism. I almost told you just how much I've been thinking about eternal things. Like my love for you. My desire to be with you. I do love you, eternally. Will you please marry me?"

My "Yes, Theo" is drowned out by the clapping, whoops, and hollers of the crowd all around us.

But as I pull him to standing and my lips close around his, I lose all awareness of that.

I'm only conscious of one thing: joy rushing through me, reverberating a heady, peaceful happiness I've never known.

Because finally, finally, I get to marry Theodore Vincent Carter.

My Theo.

***

Merre

It's all very picturesque, the scene in front of me. People at the Charles Dickens Christmas Festival have gathered around, and many of us know what's about to happen.

Aria doesn't.

At least, I hope she doesn't have any idea.

It was hard for Camilla, Howard, and me to keep it a secret these last couple of weeks at the bakeshop in the mornings. But we pulled it off, never mentioning what her boyfriend, Theo, had been scheming up. It was close a couple of times, but we managed.

And now, here we are, the festival videographer capturing everything. As soon as Theo pops the question and Aria says yes, Camilla and I will start passing out shortbread wrapped in jingle bell-topped bags. Jesse will play a medley of Aria's favorite upbeat Christmas songs over the sound system, and we'll have a big celebration.

There's a lot to celebrate, actually. I finished pastry school in the spring, and recently received my certification in baking, which means I've been able to help Camilla expand. Plus, I'm boarding a plane in a few hours to go back to my family in Plano, Texas for Christmas.

"It's snowing," one of the children nearby announces right as Theo steps out to the middle of the room, beckoning Aria to join him. I glance out the window to see the fluffy, white snow gently falling.

It's perfect. All of it. And because I'm sentimental when it comes to weddings and mushy love stuff, a ball forms in my throat.

All around the grand foyer, the growing crowd watches on. There's a mix of people who are here for the engagement and those who happened to be at the festival as it winds down for the year.

A waving hand on the opposite side of the foyer catches my attention. The man, mid-twenties with dark hair, is staring right at me, his expression one of surprise. I begin to lift a hand to wave back to be polite when it hits me.

He mouths, "Merry?"

Instead of waving, I run a hand through my hair and turn my attention back to Theo, who's now down on one knee.

I will not wave at that man. I will not give him the time of day. Waving at him, giving him the time of day, would mean I've accepted the past.

I have not.

Because now I know exactly who he is. Why he's here, I have no idea. I'd be less shocked if the King of England himself decided to come celebrate this Dickensian festival with us lowly Coloradans.

It's Noah.

Noah Elliot.

And I swore years ago I'd never speak to him again.

Don't miss Merre's story in *A Red Velvet Christmas*, coming Winter 2024. https://www.amazon.com/dp/B0BR64C1BV

Howard Beckwith's Raspberry Swirl Cheesecake

Ingredients:

½ C. butter, melted, plus more for the pan

1 ½ C. graham cracker crumbs

3 (8 oz.) packages cream cheese, softened

1 C. plus 4 T. granulated sugar, divided

1 C. sour cream

3 large eggs, room temperature

1 pinch salt

2 t. real vanilla extract

Juice and zest of one lemon

1 ½ C. raspberries

Boiling water

Directions:

Preheat oven to 350 degrees. Butter the bottom and sides of a 9 inch pie pan (or a springform pan lined with foil). Zest one lemon and set aside.

Mix graham cracker crumbs, melted butter, and 2 T. sugar in medium bowl. Press mixture into the bottom and sides of the pie pan.

Bake for 10 minutes and let cool on a wire rack. Reduce oven temperature to 325 degrees.

Prepare raspberry puree by processing the raspberries in a food processor until smooth. Strain through a fine wire mess colander and discard solids. Mix 2 T. sugar and the juice of one lemon into the raspberry liquid and set aside.

In a large bowl, use an electric mixer to beat the cream cheese and sugar until smooth, about 4 minutes. Beat in the sour cream until blended. Add the eggs one at a time, beating well after each addition. Mix in the salt, vanilla, and lemon zest.

Pour roughly half of the cream cheese mixture into the pie pan with the cooled graham cracker crust. Spoon one-fourth of the raspberry sauce onto the cheesecake in stripes. Pour the rest of the cream cheese mixture on top. Spoon the remaining raspberry sauce onto the top of the cheesecake in circles. Using a butter knife, gently swish through the cheesecake, making the raspberry sauce swirl.

Place cheesecake in a large, shallow roasting pan or cake pan, then place in oven. Gently pour or ladle boiling water into the pan until it reaches halfway up the sides of the cheesecake.

Bake (about 60 to 70 minutes) until the cheesecake is set around the edges but still wobbly in the center (the wobbly portion should be about the size of a silver dollar). Cool completely on a wire rack, then wrap tightly in saran wrap. Store in refrigerator at least five hours. Let the cheesecake rest at room temperature for 30 minutes before slicing and serving.

Author's Note

Over a year ago, during a family get-together at our new house, my nephew shared a funny story. As I listened, I knew it had to make it in one of my books someday.

"Someday" came sooner than I expected, as the relationship between the characters of Theo and Aria (brother and best friend, respectively, of the main characters in book one of the series, *A Shortbread Christmas*) took on a saucy tone. You see, my nephew's story wove itself around the way Theo and Aria interacted with one another. Thus, a catalytic scene in *A Cheesecake Christmas* (the one involving a redhead and a bottle of water in the bakeshop!) was born.

As always, I thank the Lord for giving me everything, including the drive to revere and create story. It's part of what makes me who I am. And because of God, I love who I am and the life that I have.

Thank you to my family. I love you. Please can we play Nuts about Mutts now that I'm done with this book?

Lindzee, when you received this manuscript, it was a royal, unlikeable mess. I appreciate you helping me see that and understand all the ways I could fix it. You made this book possible.

Linda and Britney, as always, your notes and suggestions were spot on and totally instrumental in making this book what it is. Thank you so very much!

Jane, Dee, and Jordan, I'm so glad you helped clean up and refine my manuscript! Your expertise is invaluable.

I'm grateful for the adorable cover, Lindzee.

To all of the other writer friends who offered their advice on my blurb and who help me market my books, I'm forever grateful.

My ARC readers and the Bookstagram community! You make this possible. YOU. What a beautiful and unexpected treasure you are.

About the Author

Deb Goodman's obsession with the written word started at age three, when she realized the old-timey newsprint wallpaper in her family's bathroom had actual words on it. The only problem? By the time she learned to read a couple of years later, the wallpaper had been replaced with something else—boring, non-worded wallpaper—and to this day, she still doesn't know what it said.

Now, she and her husband and four children live in Utah. They love sports, music, and doing slightly insulting, pretend voices for their little shorkie, Mavis.

Deb writes funny, small-town romance that you won't need to shield your kids' eyes from. Writing lovey dovey books comes naturally to Deb since, to her, there's nothing better than reading and writing about how two people fall in love.

Love truly does make the world go 'round.

Connect with her!

Newsletter: https://bit.ly/3DtjNSU

Website: https://debgoodmanwrites.com

Amazon: https://www.amazon.com/stores/Deb-Goodman/author/B07L4YL1CL

Instagram: https://instagram.com/debgoodmanwrites

TikTok handle: @debgoodmanauthor

Facebook: https://www.facebook.com/debgoodmanwrites

BookBub: https://www.bookbub.com/authors/deb-goodman